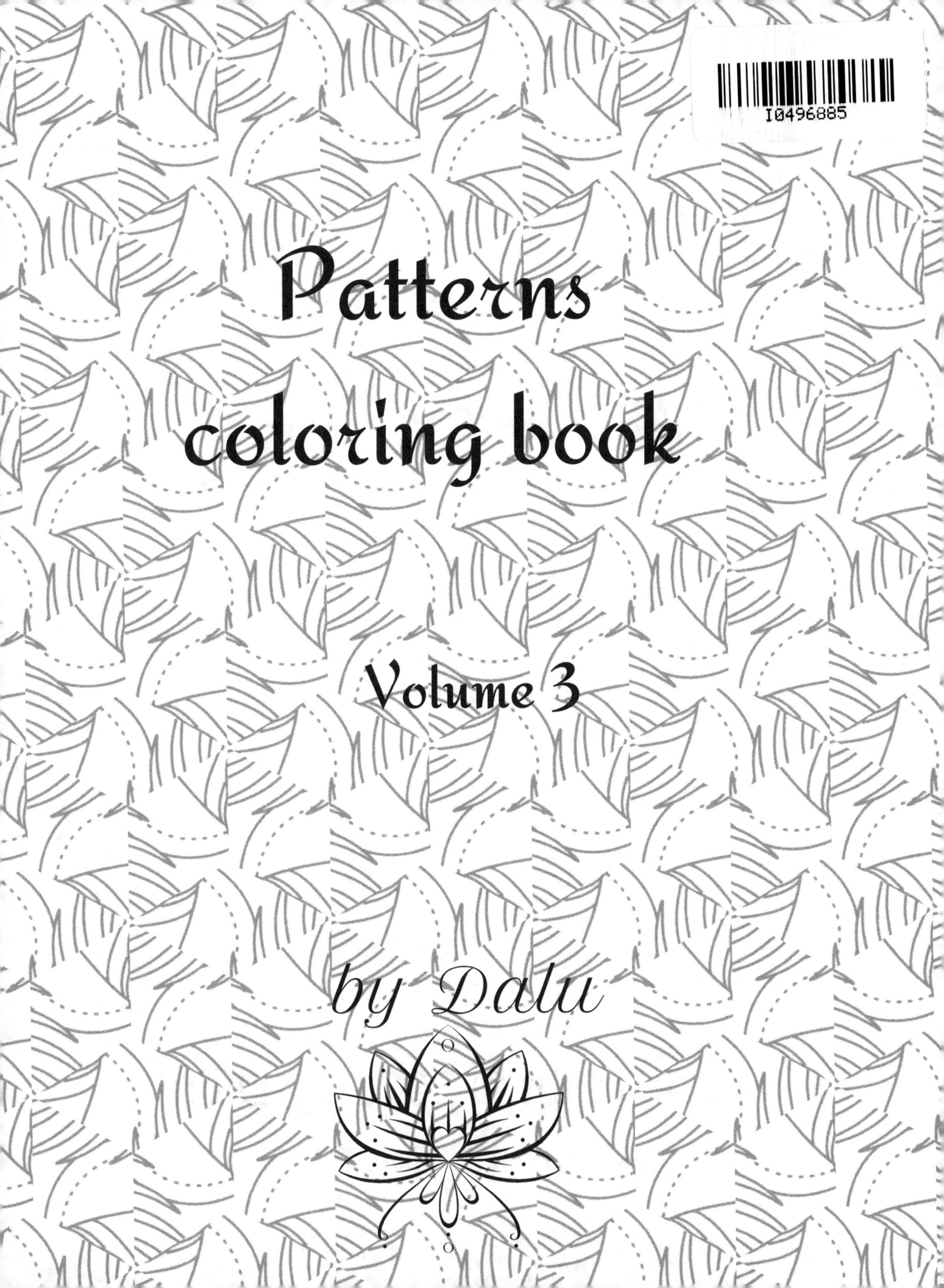

Patterns coloring book

Volume 3

by Dalu

Copyright © 2021 by Dalu
All rights reserved

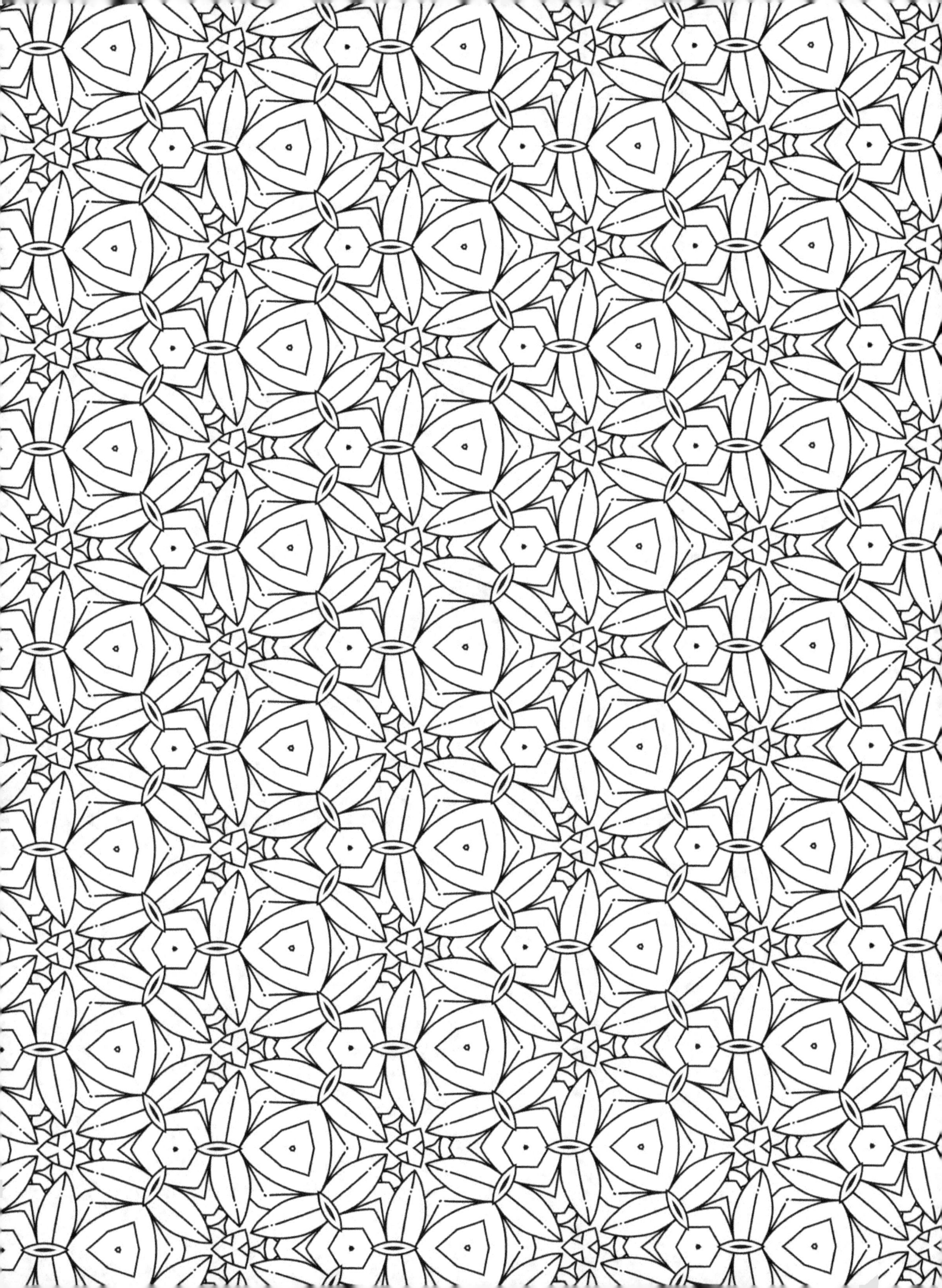

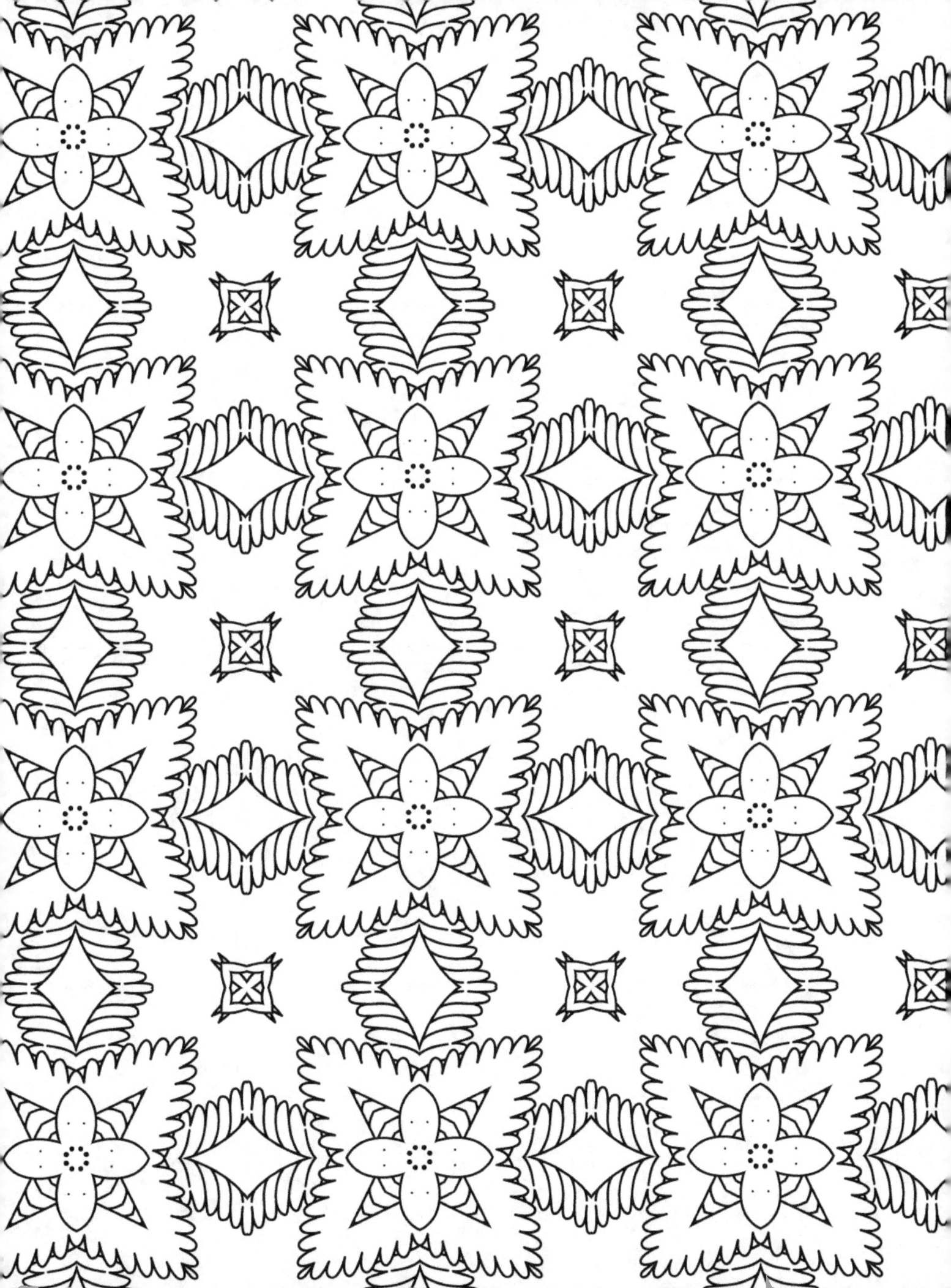

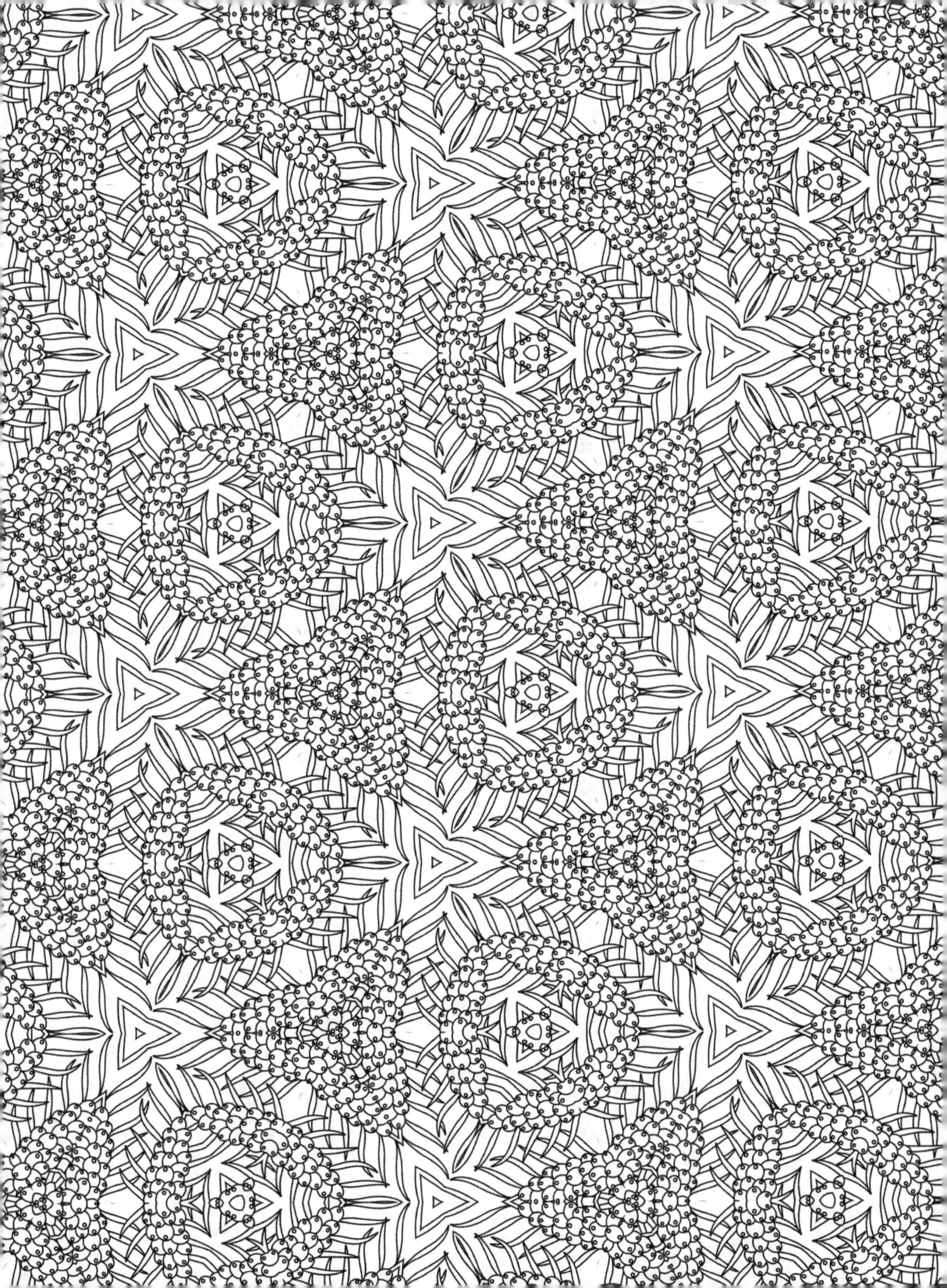

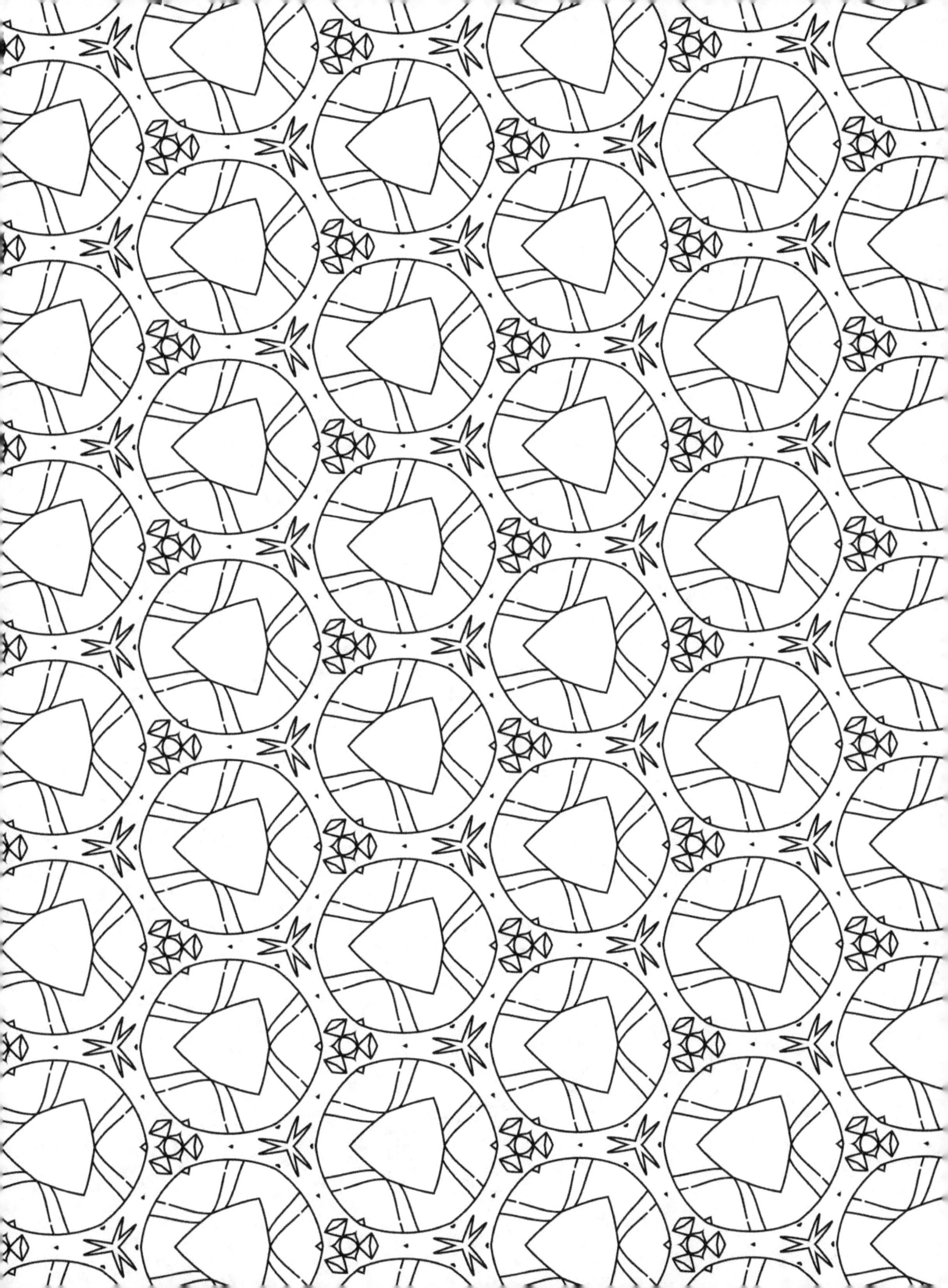

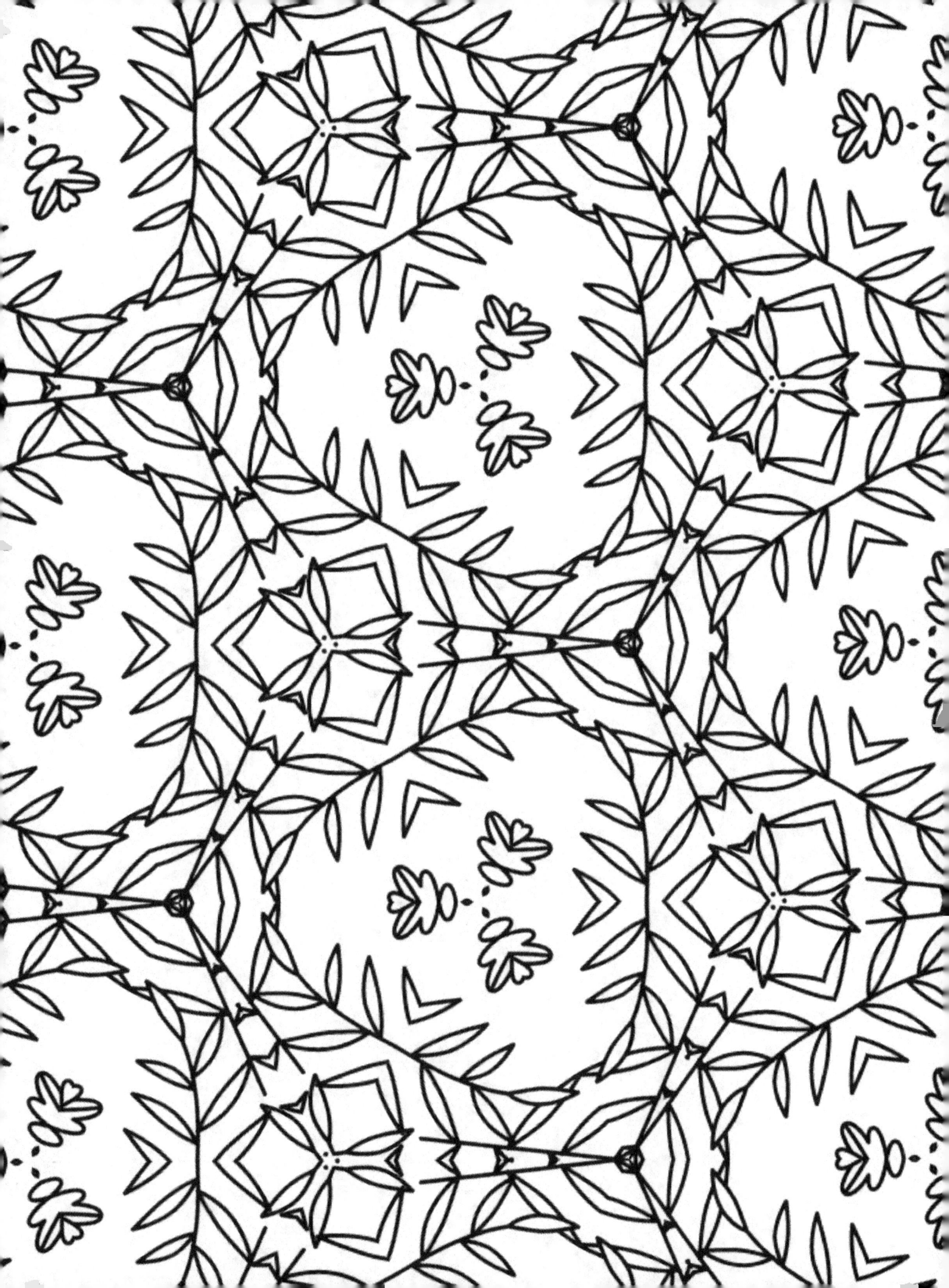

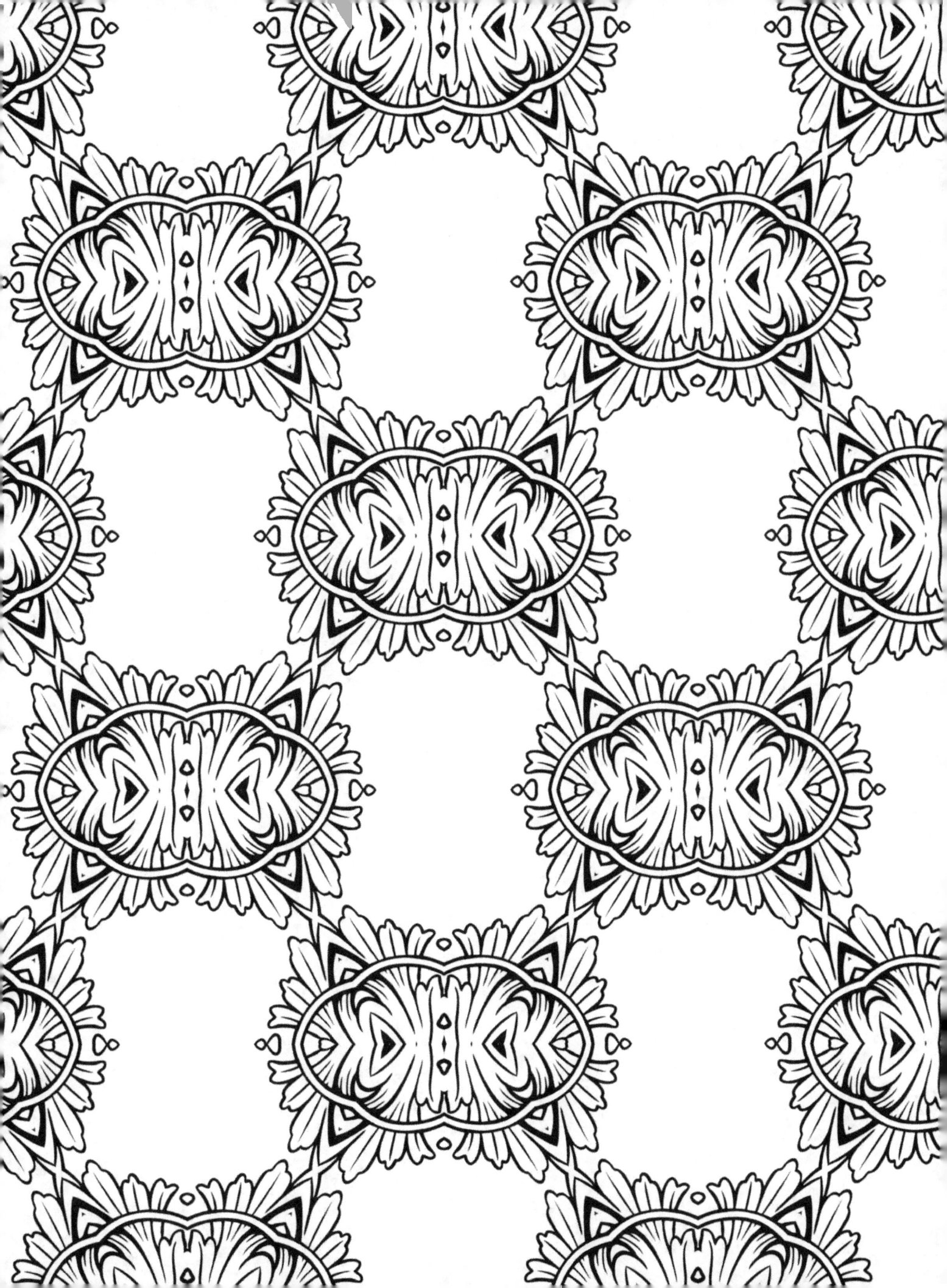

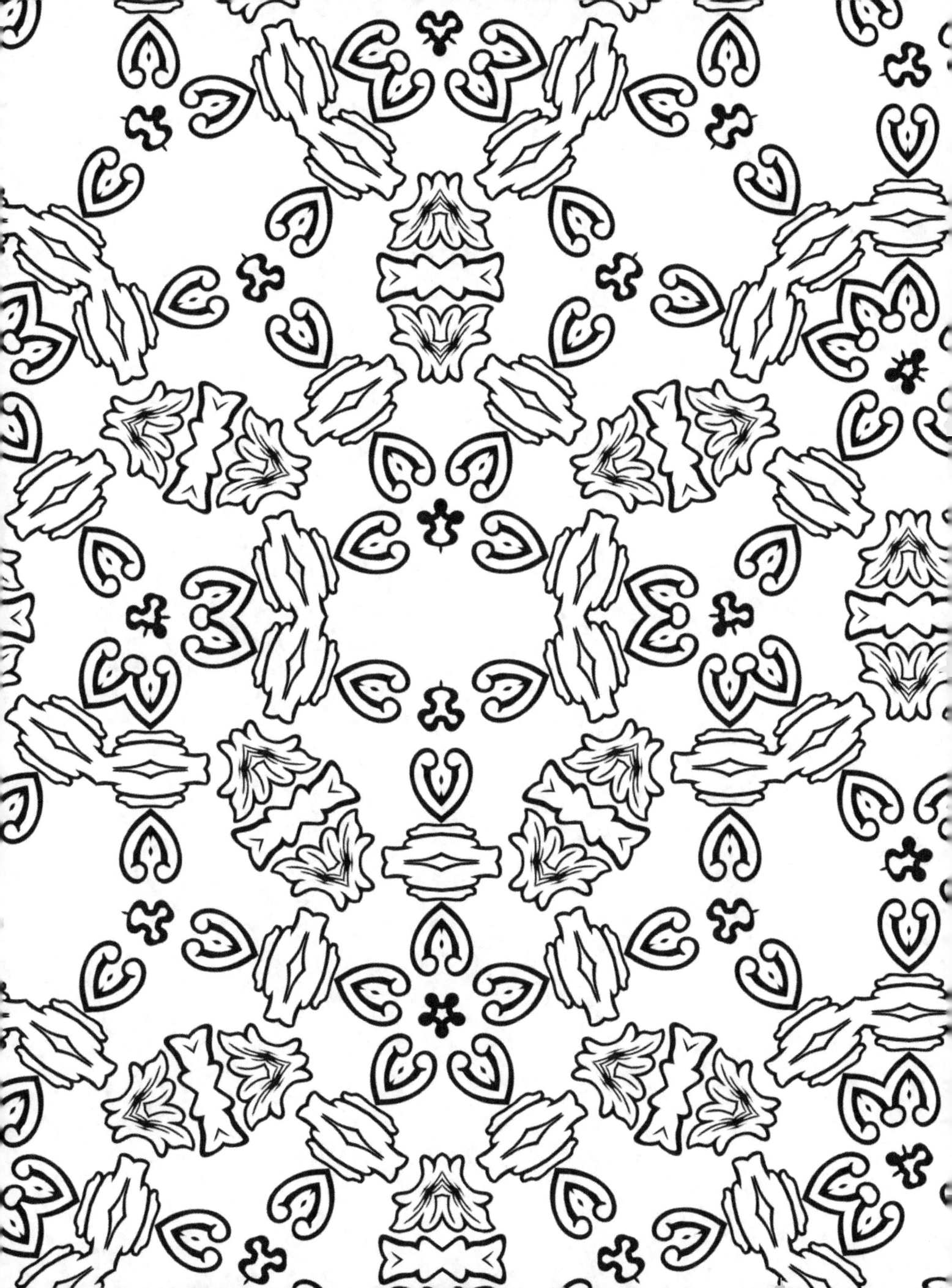

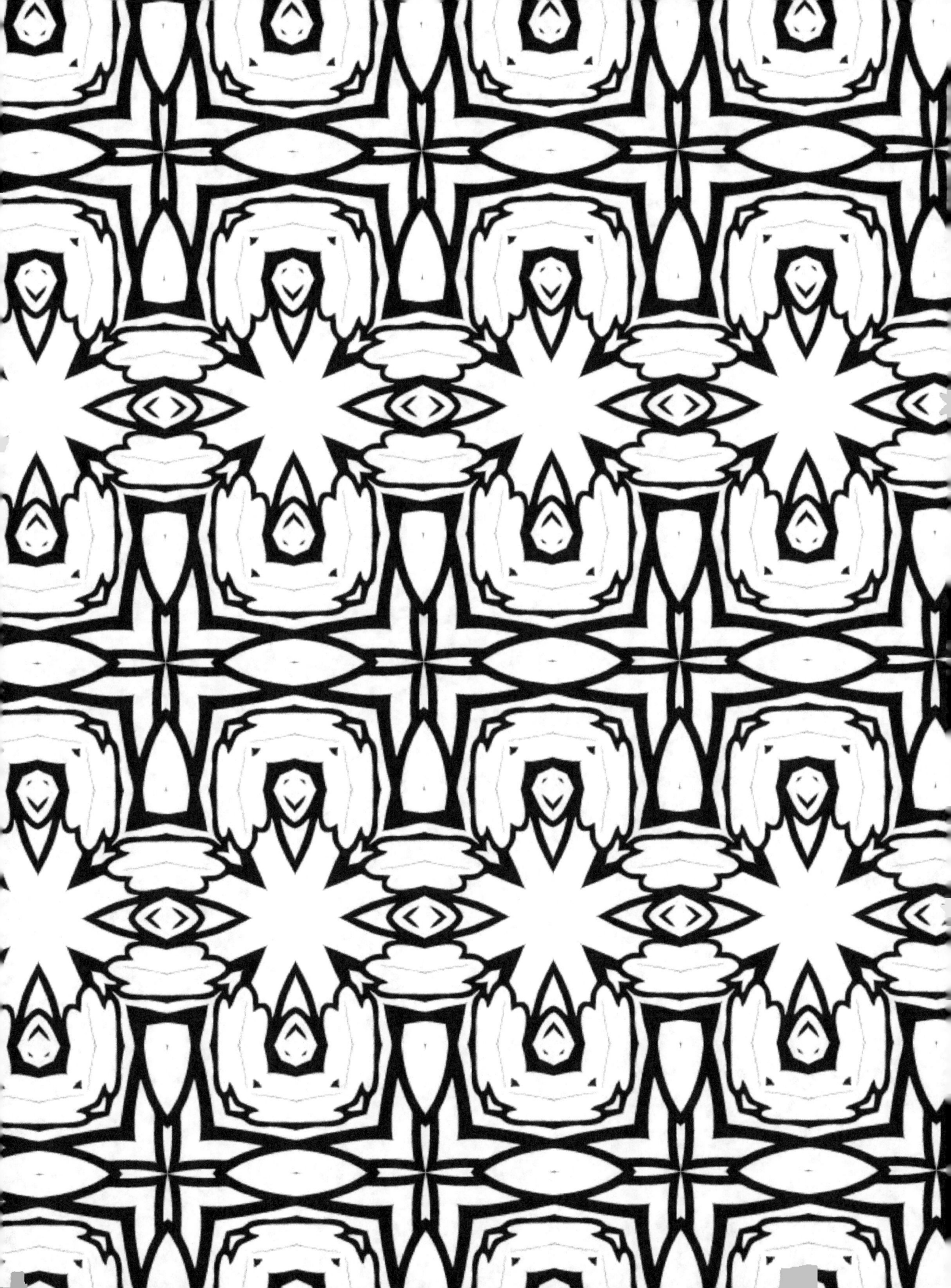

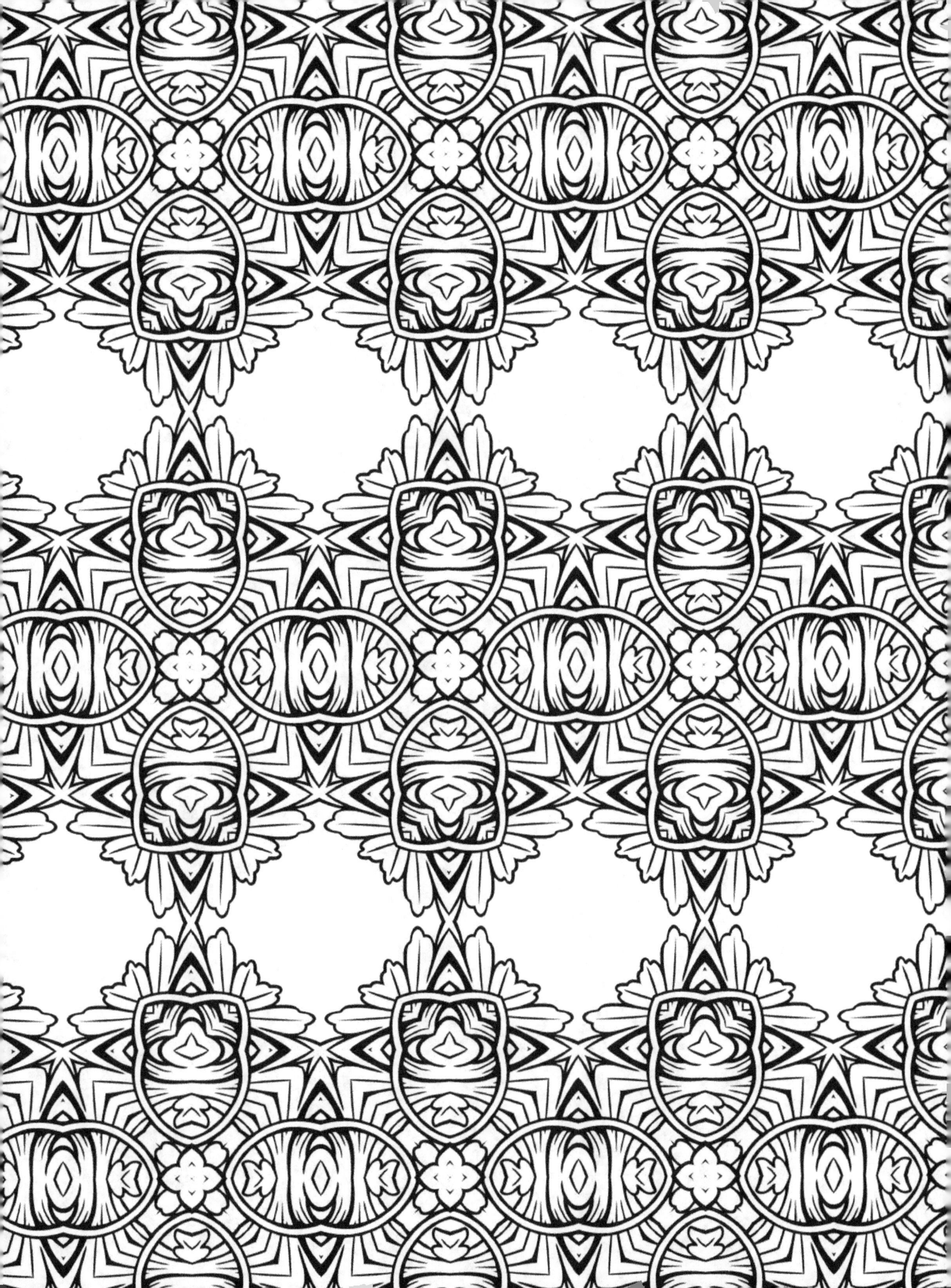

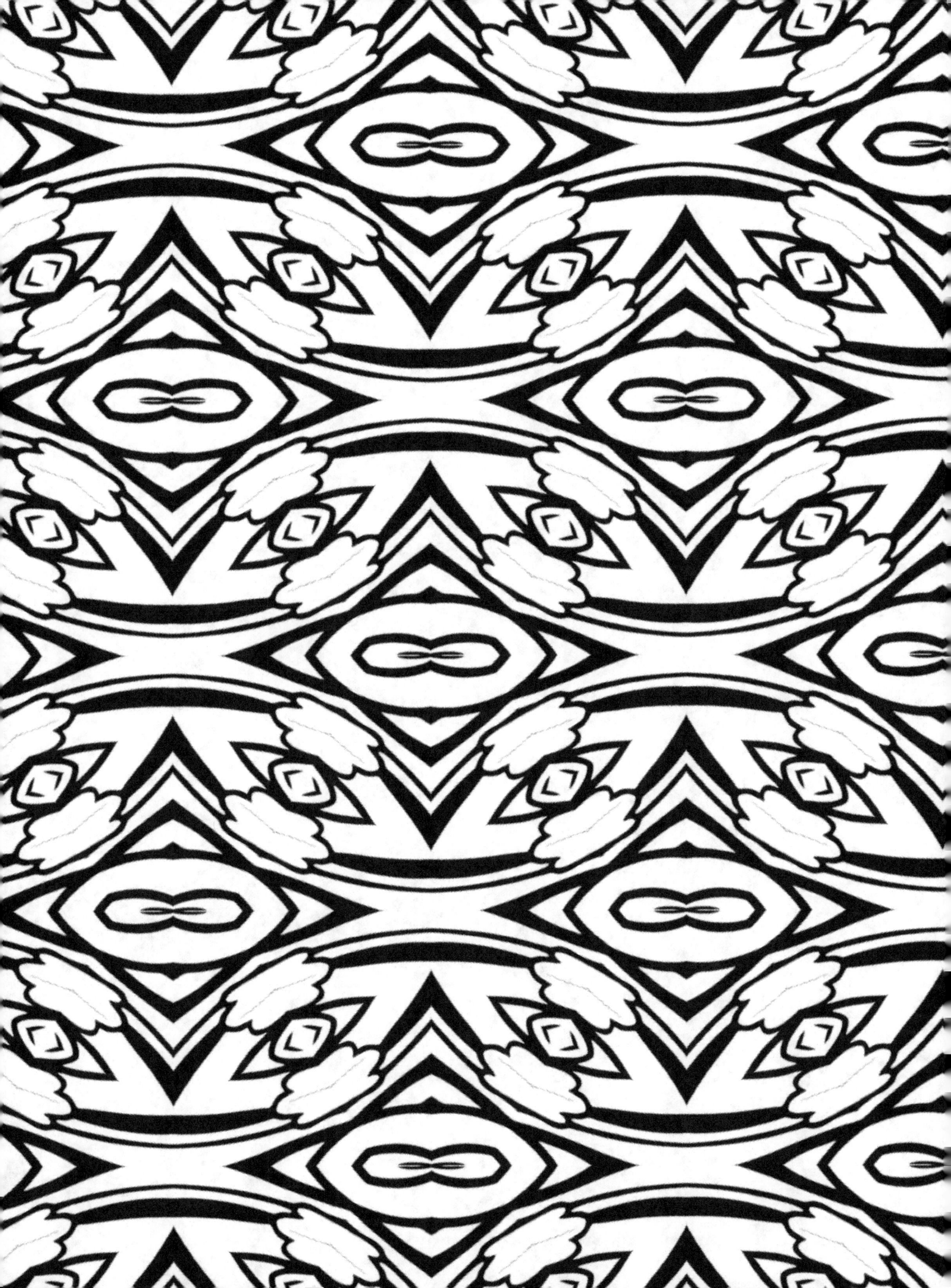

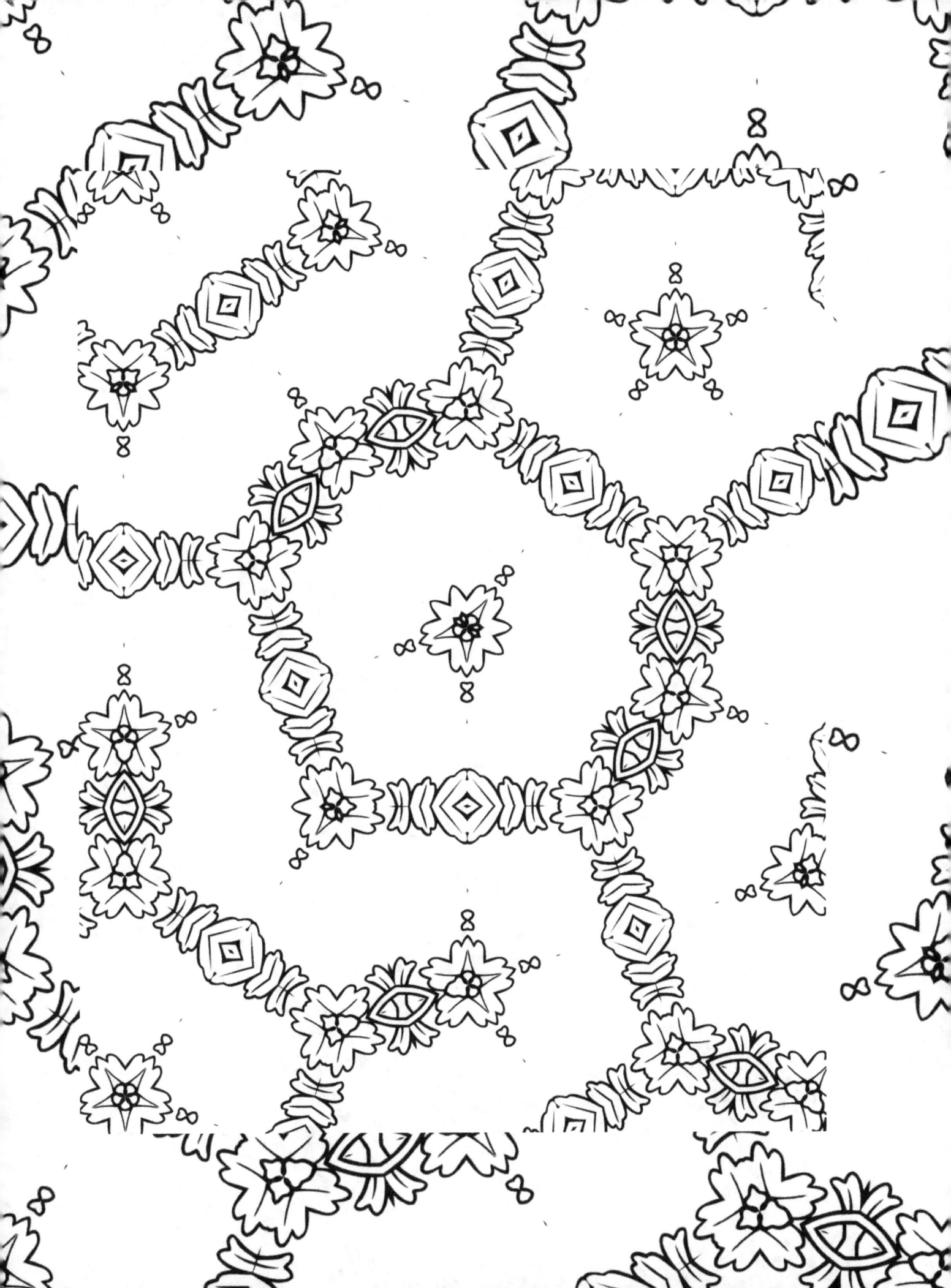

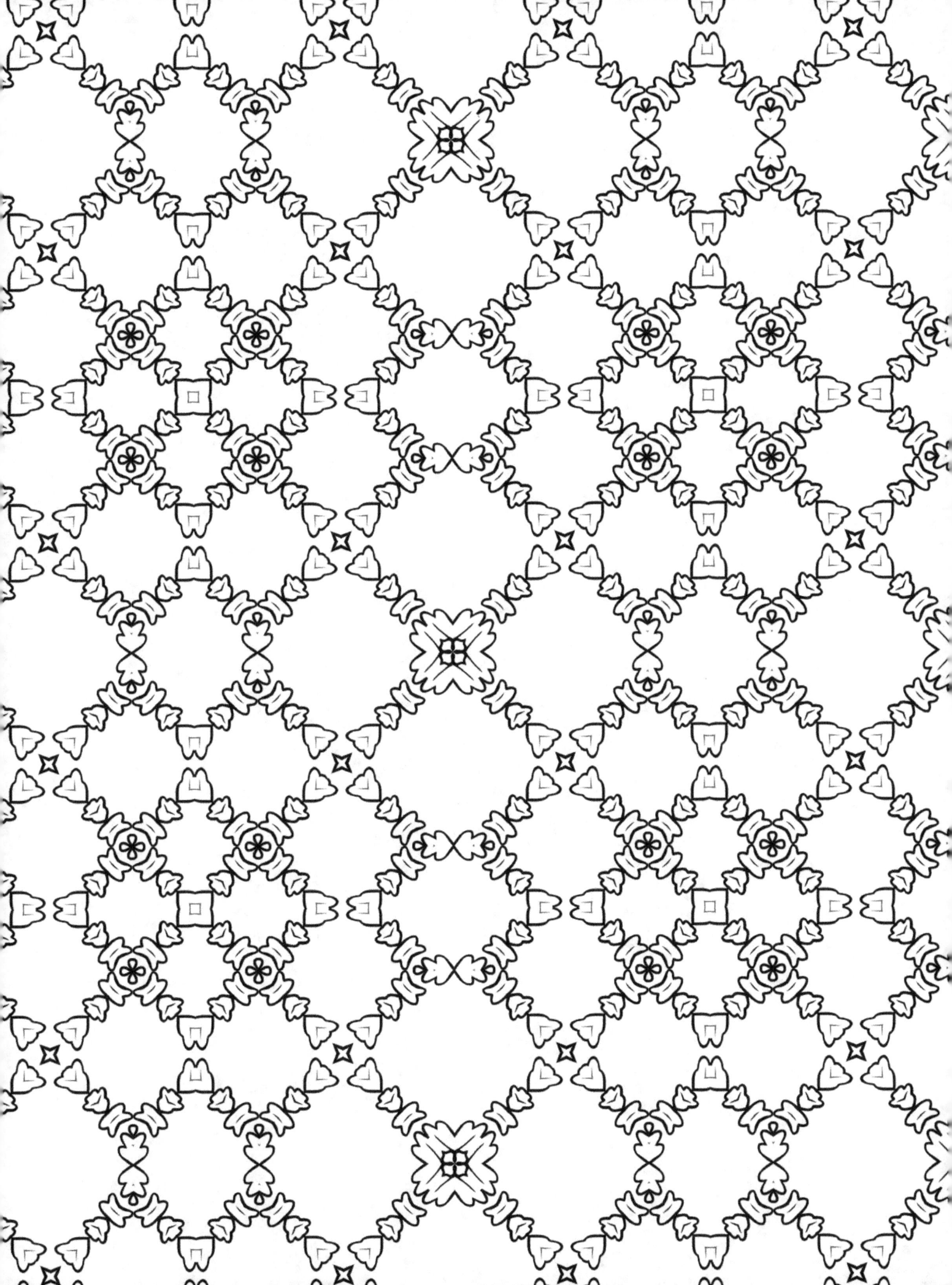

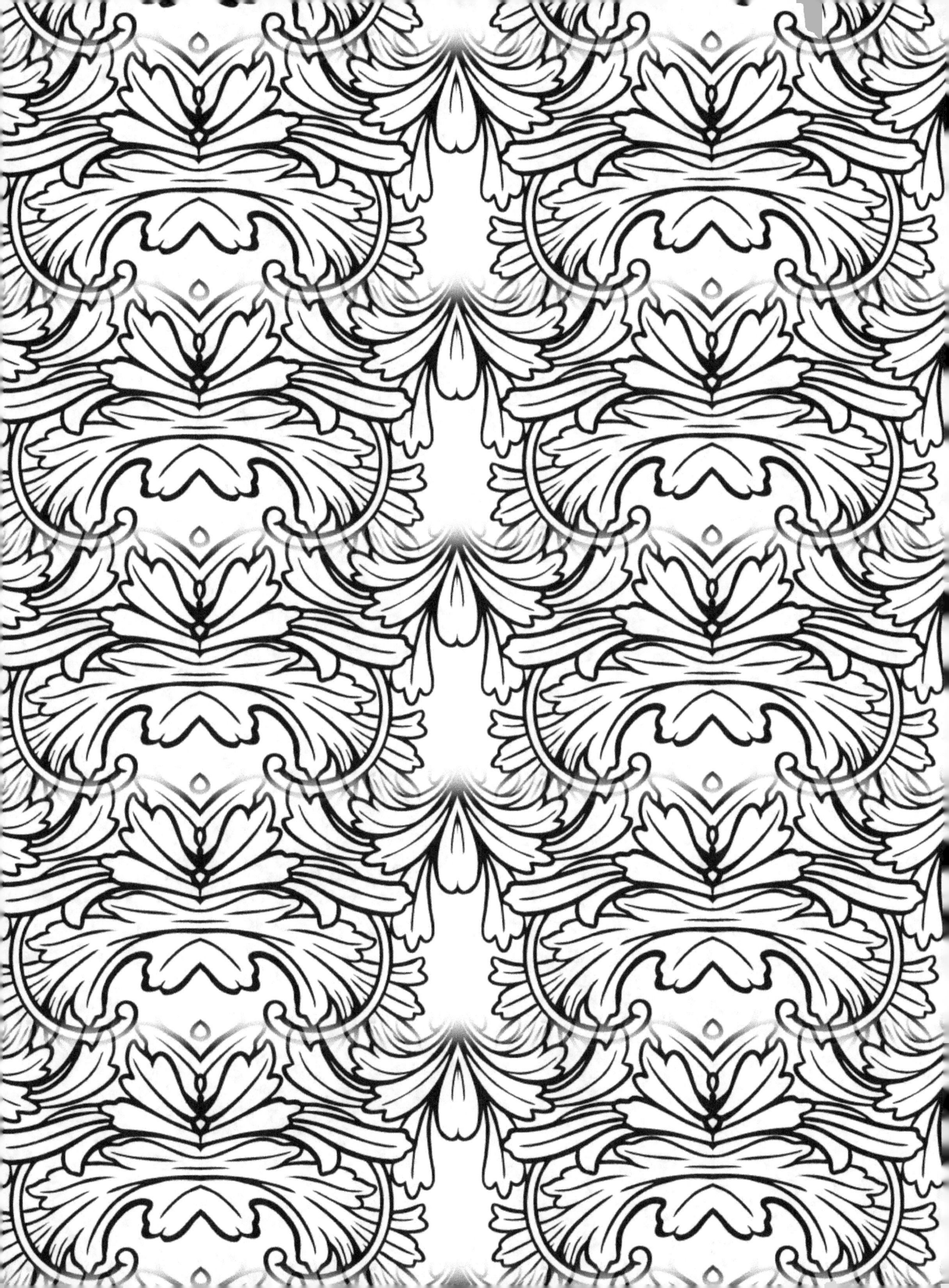

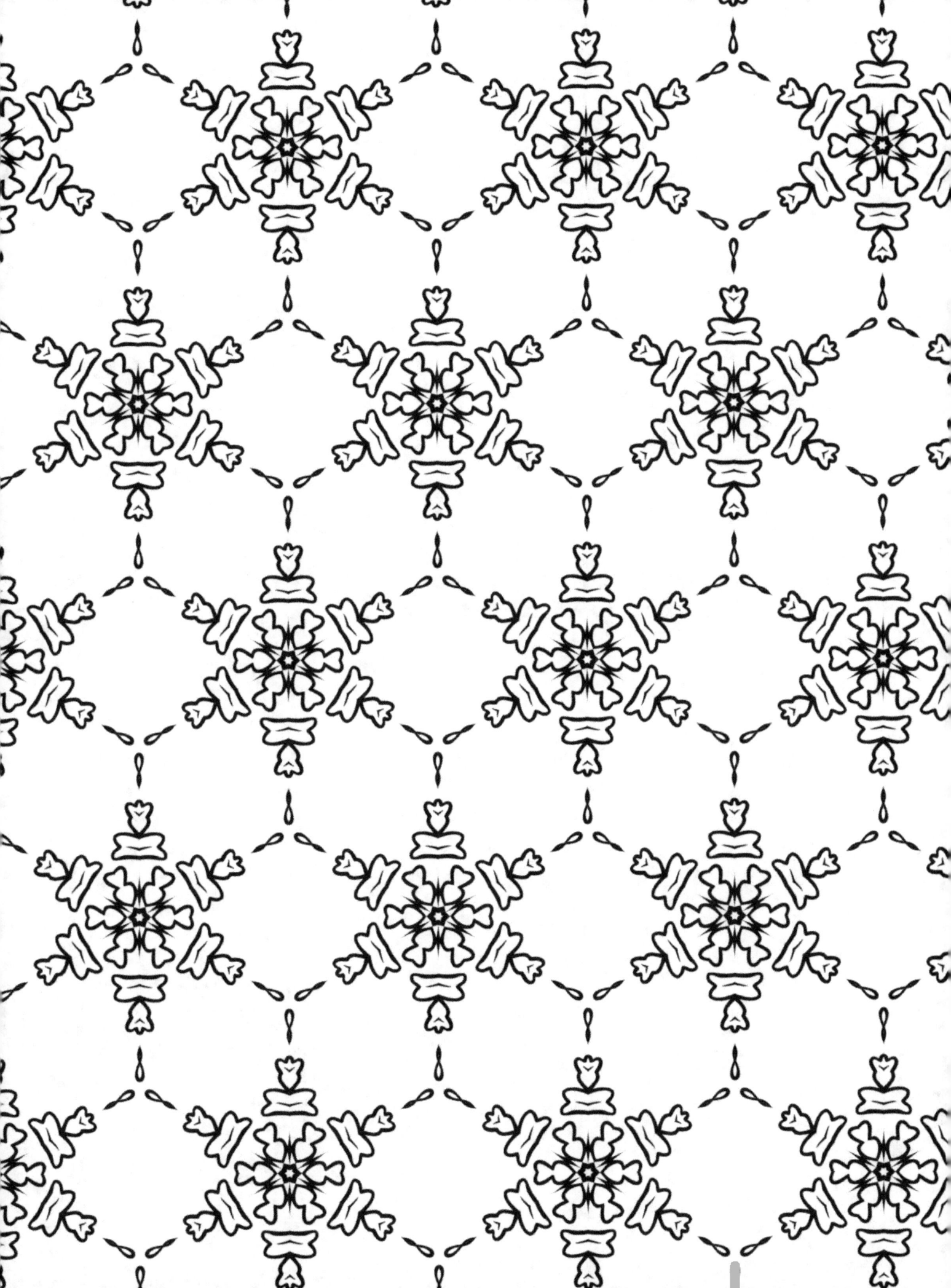

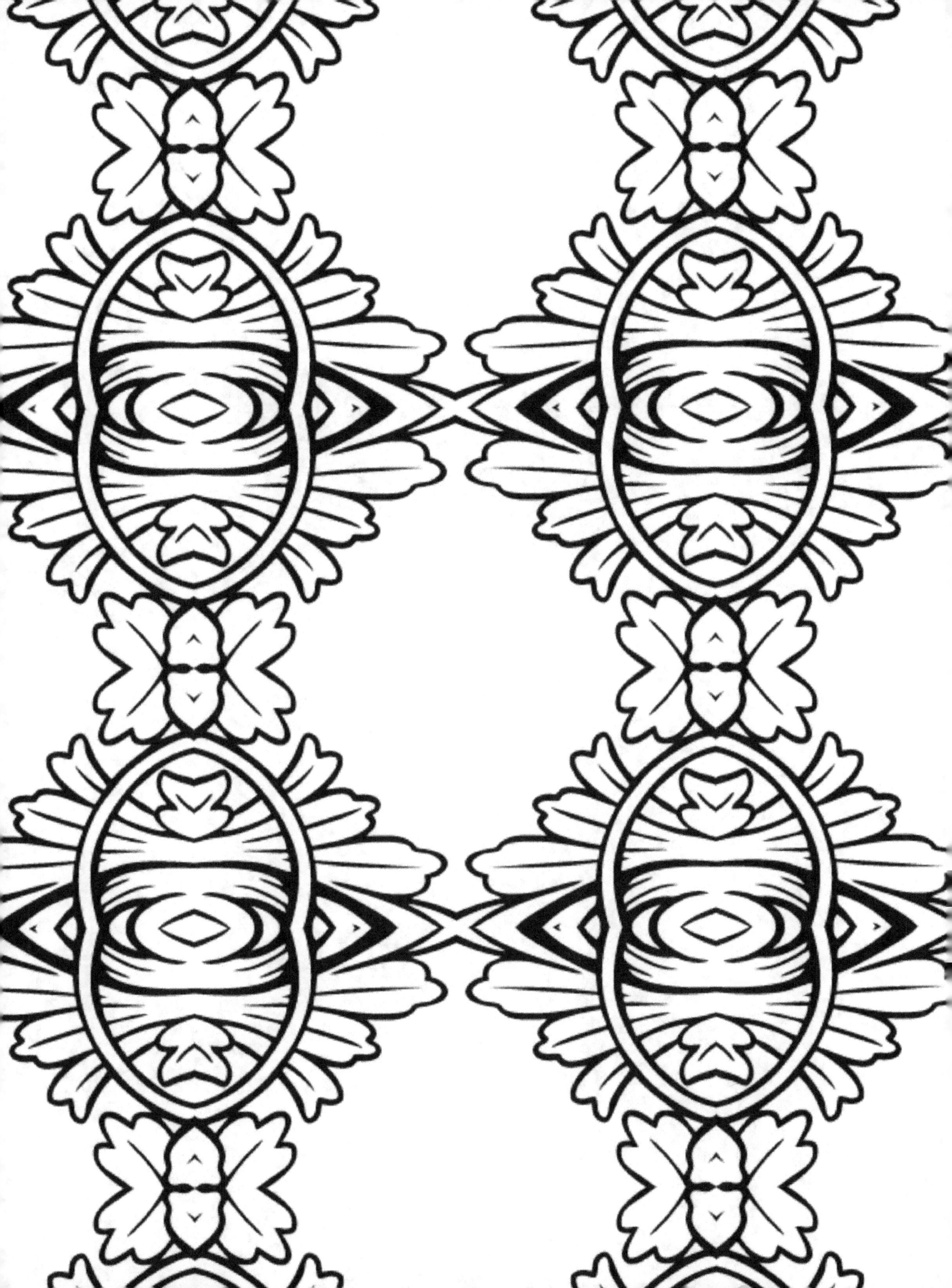

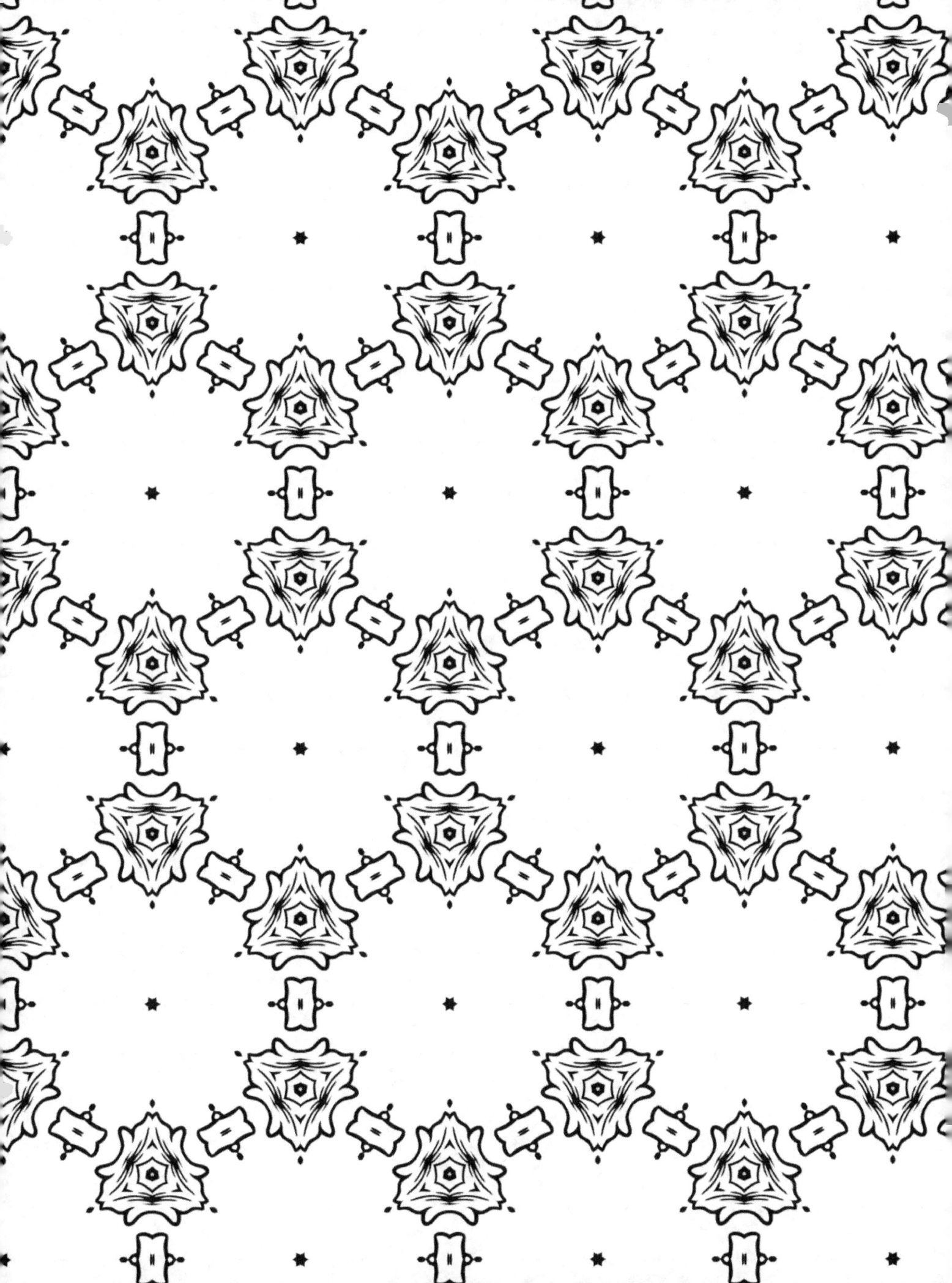

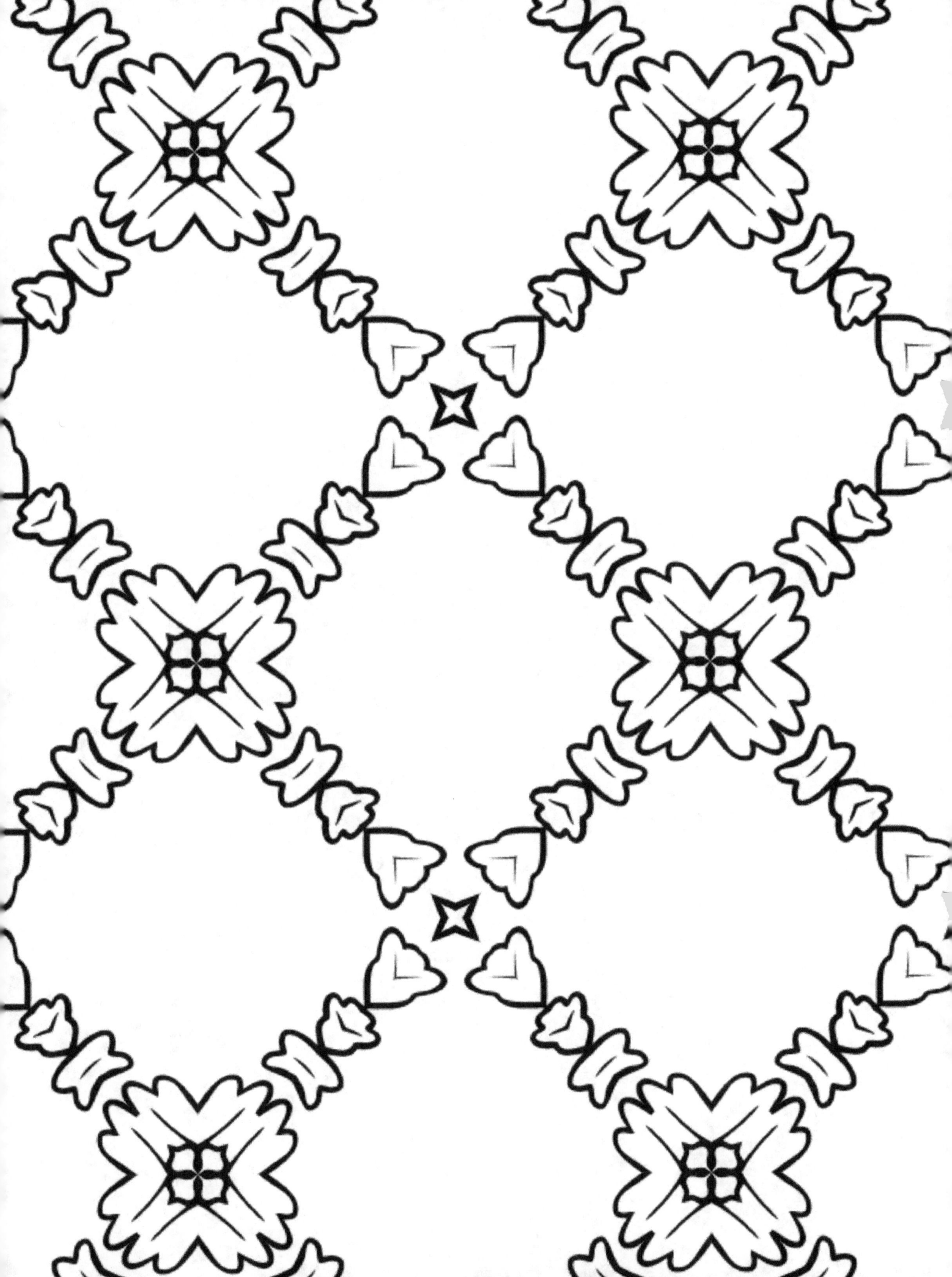

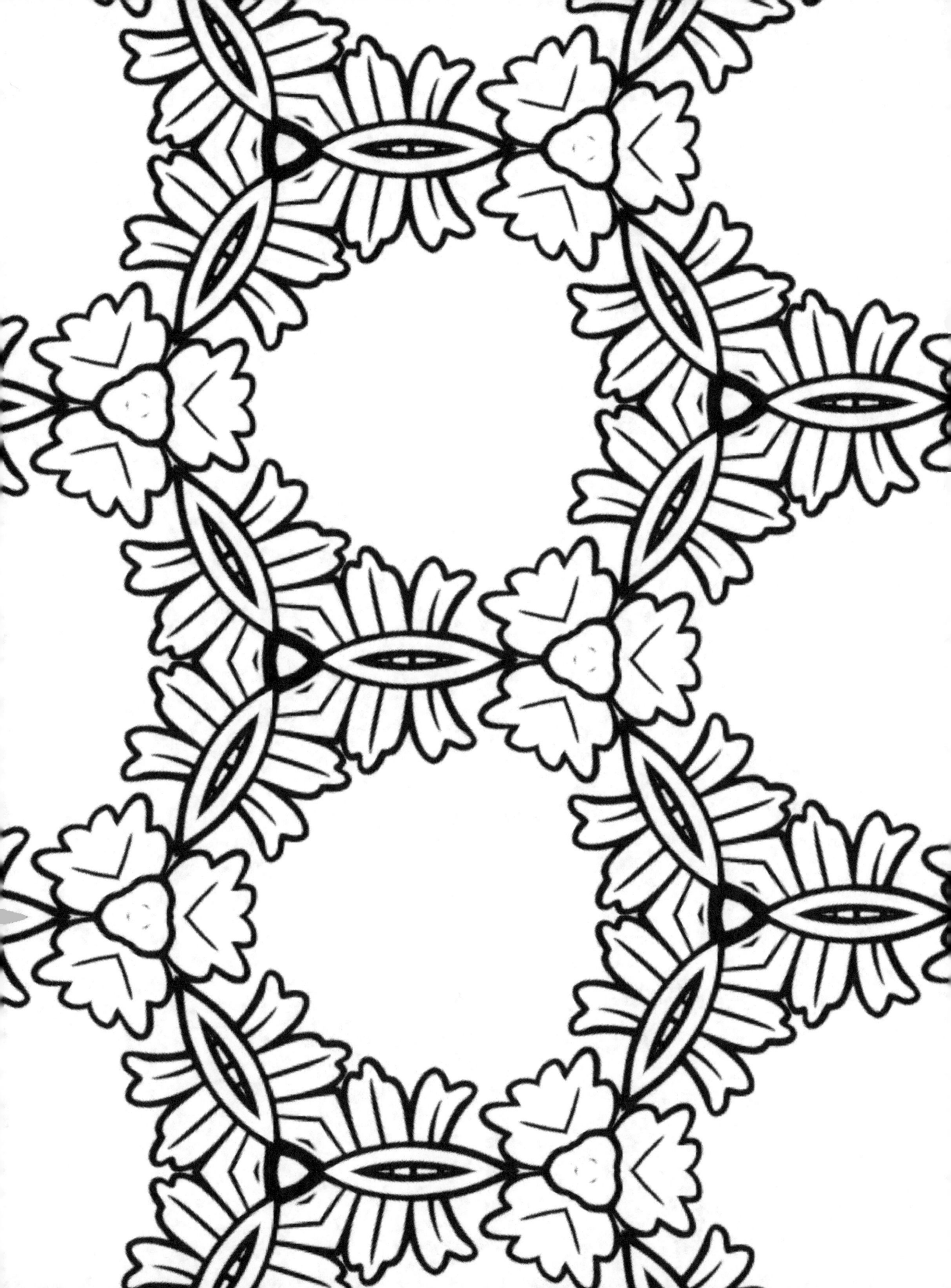

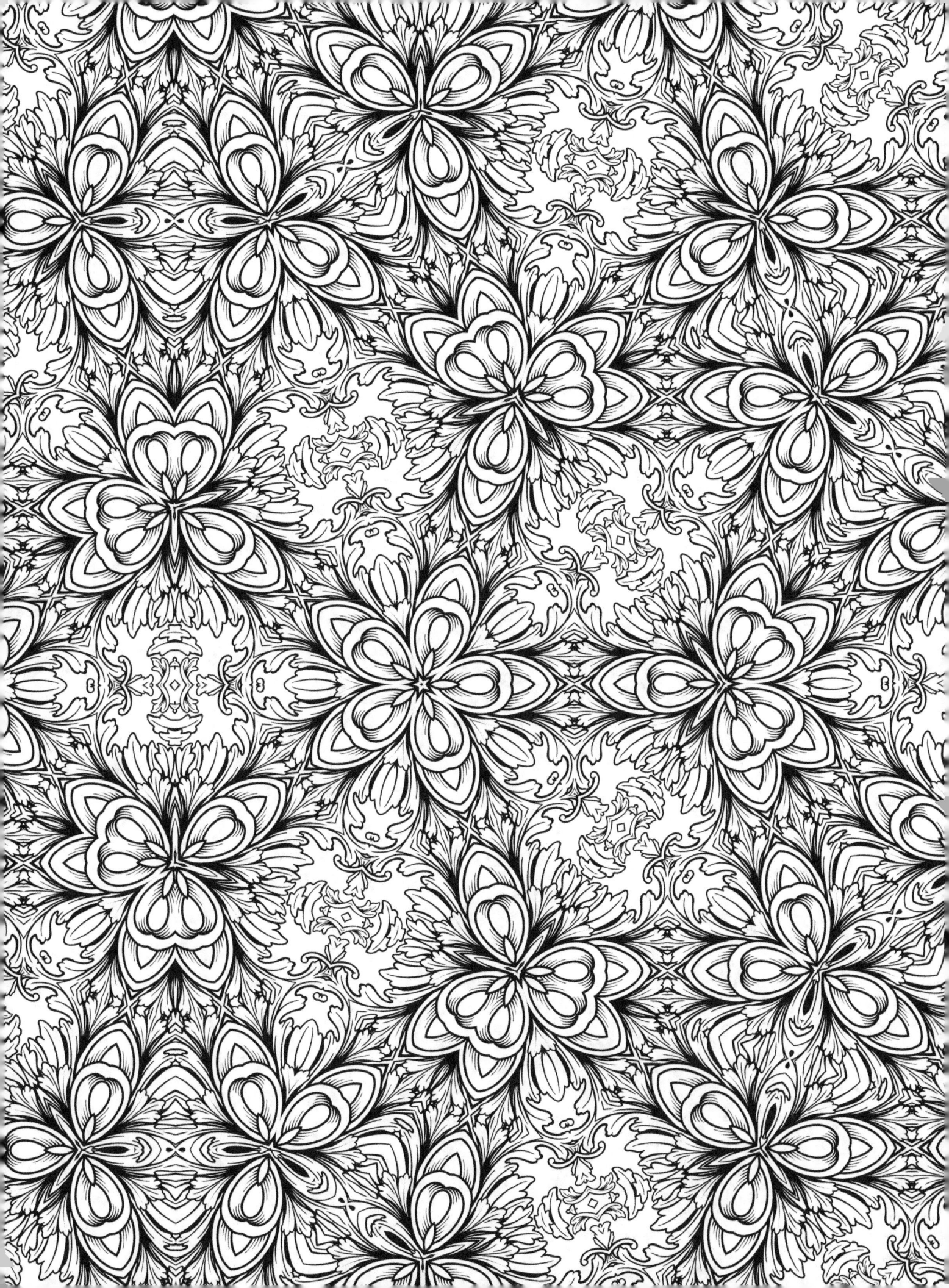

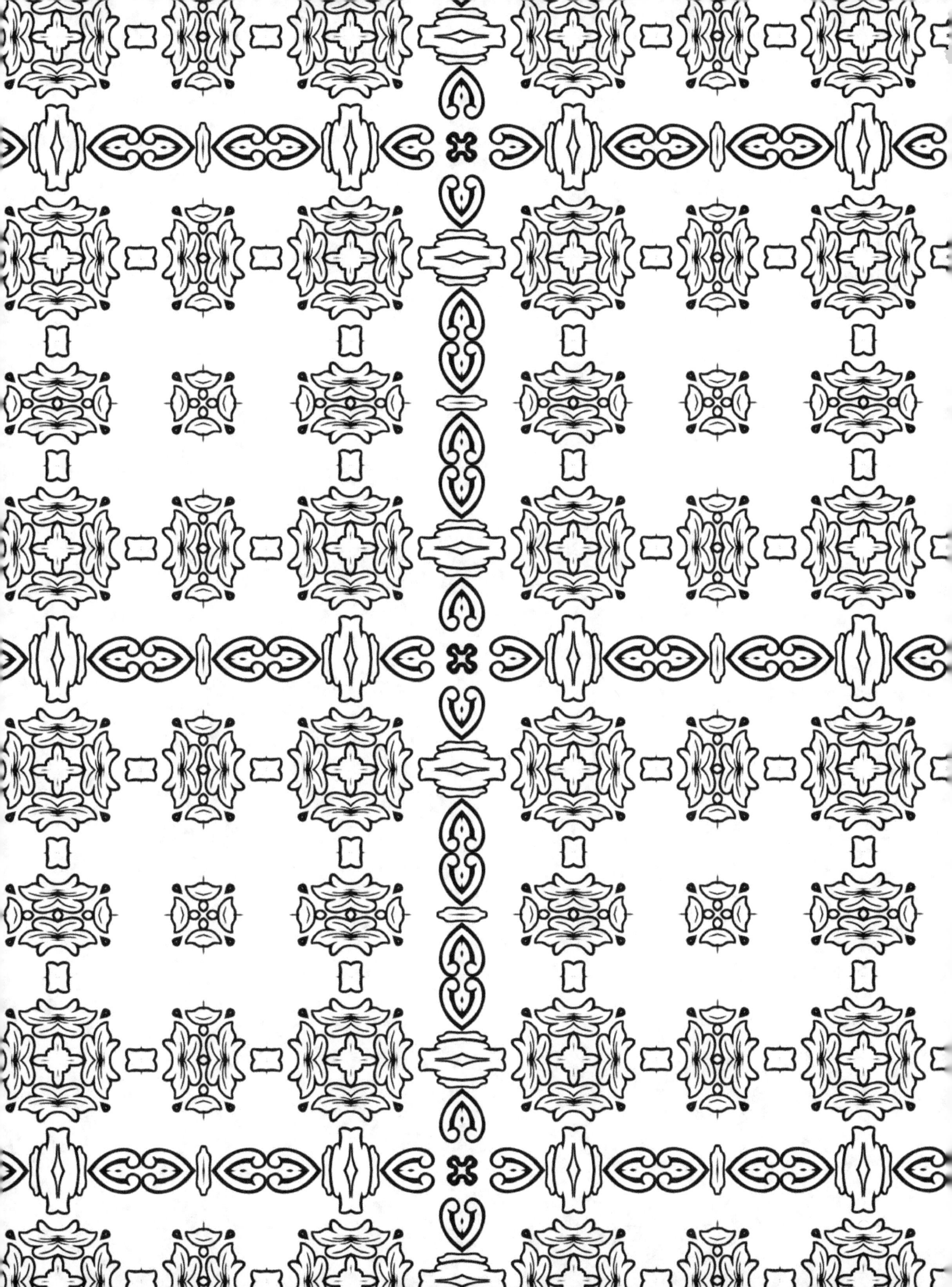

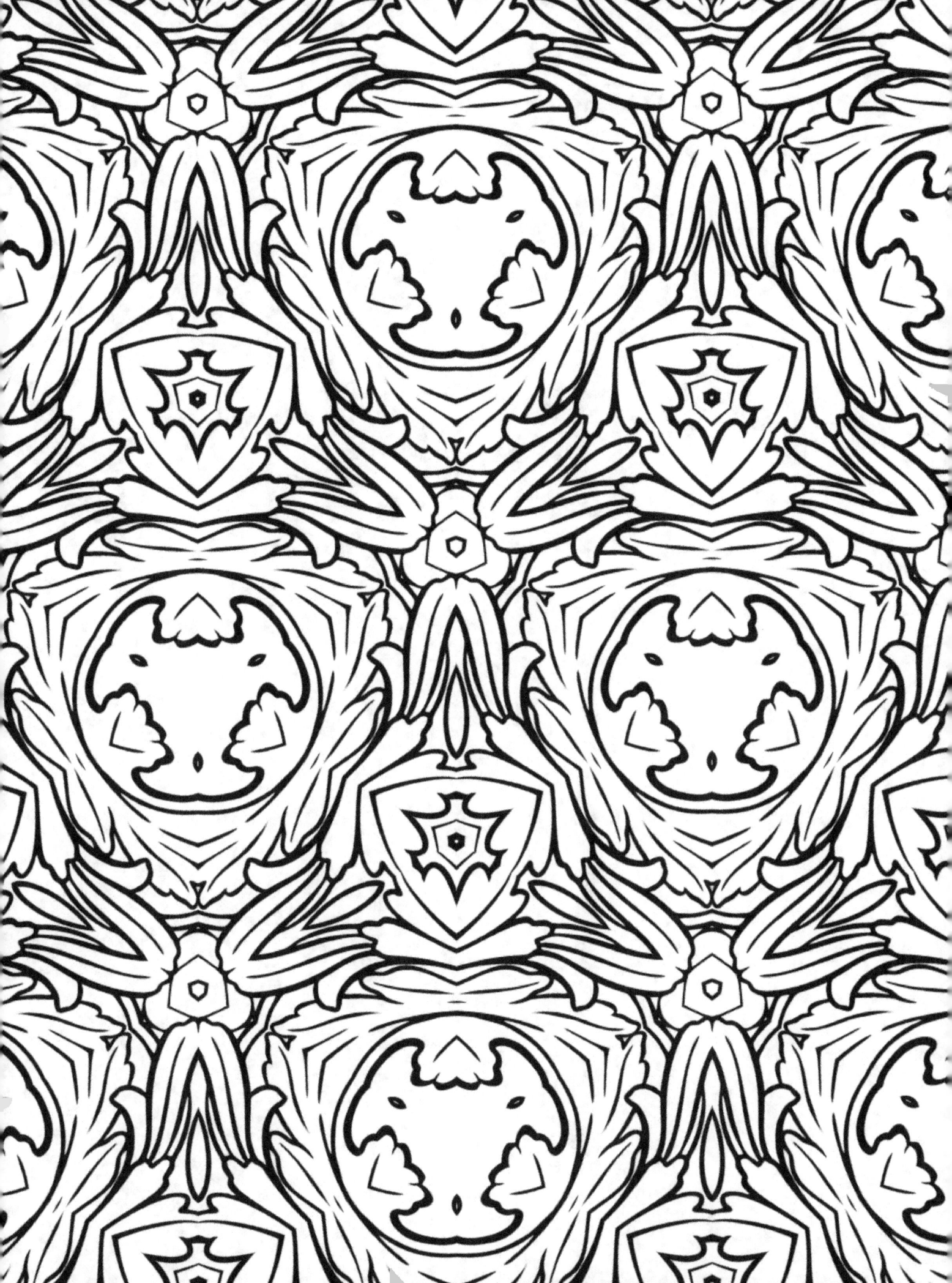

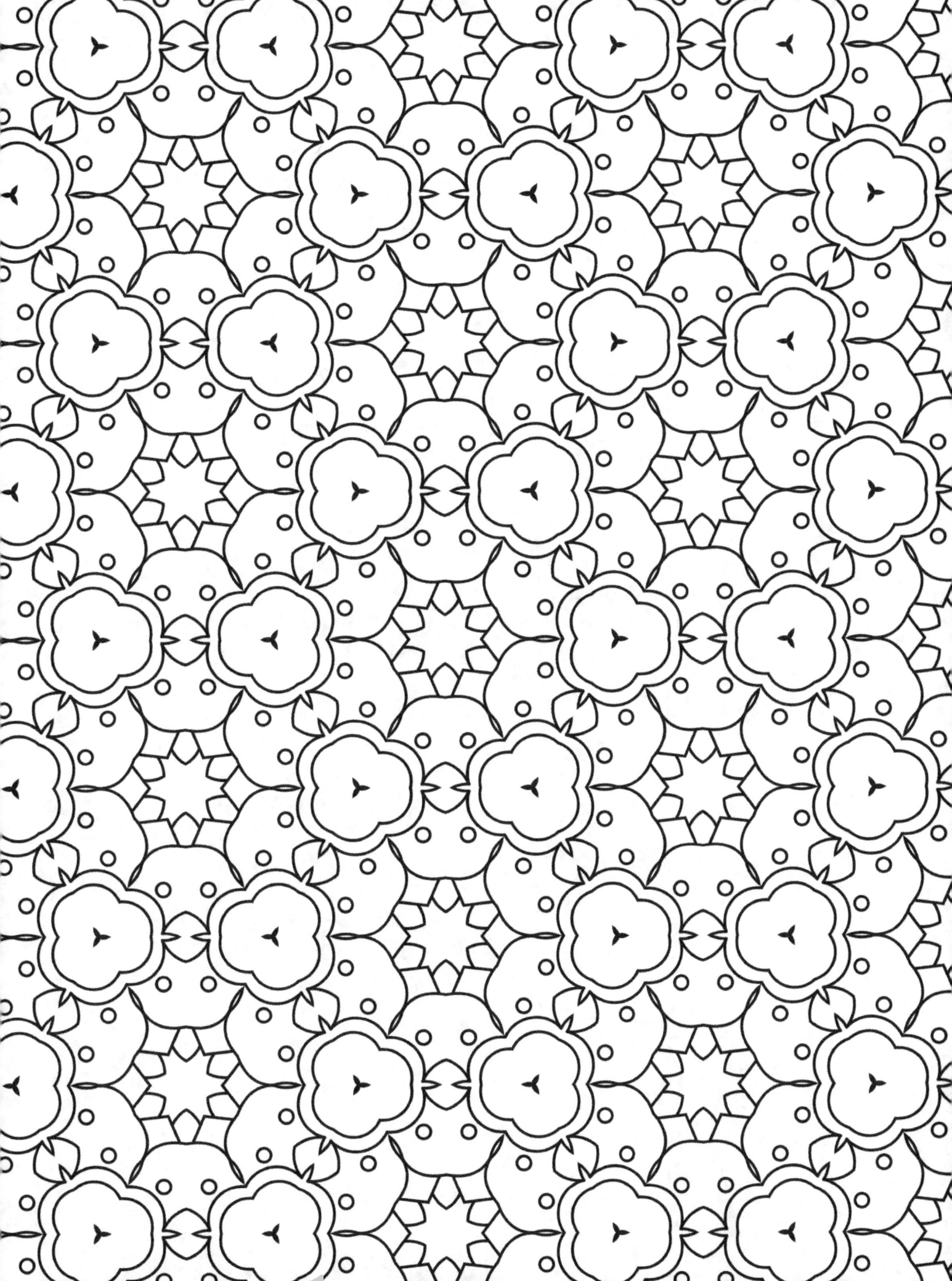

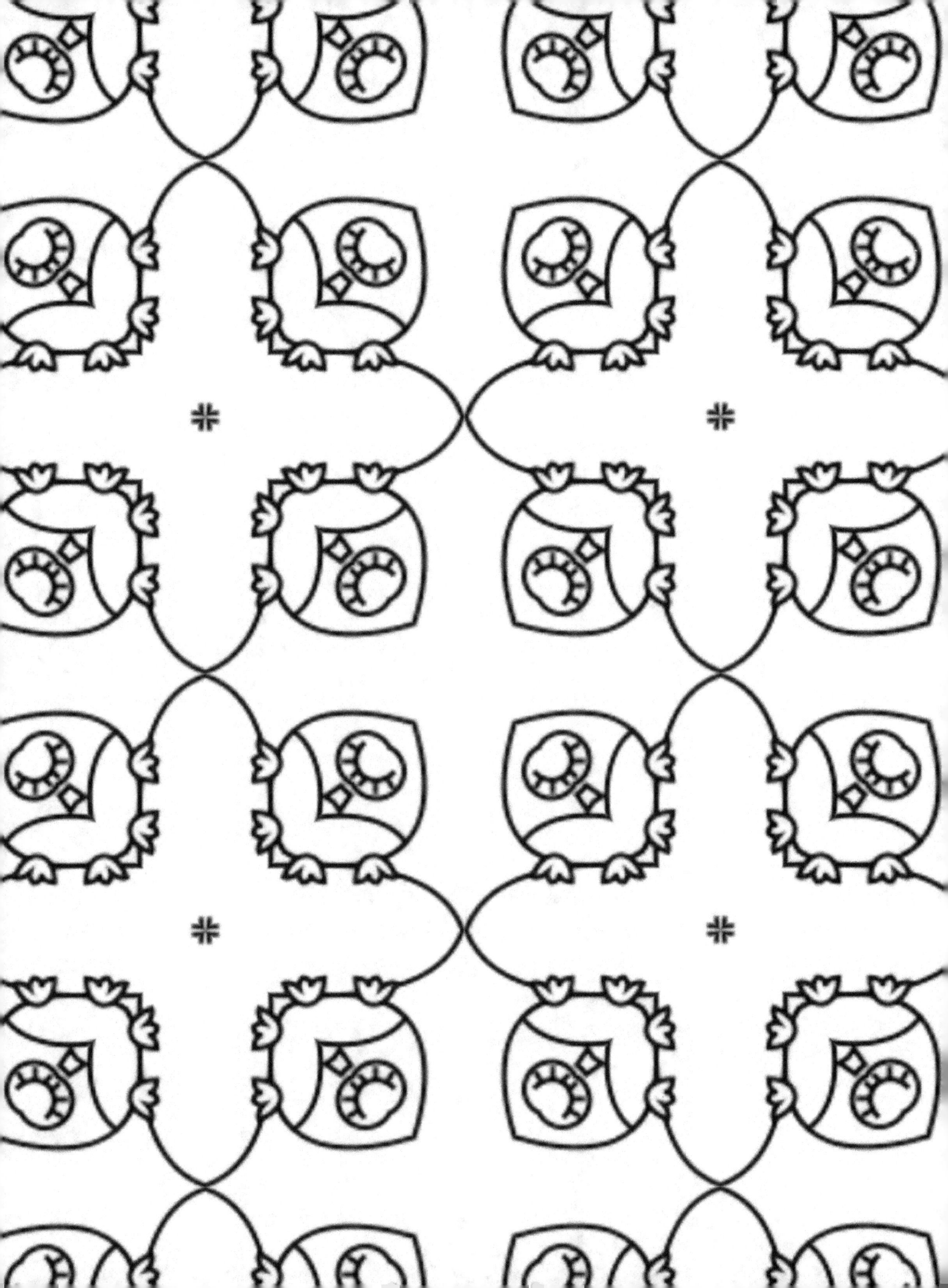

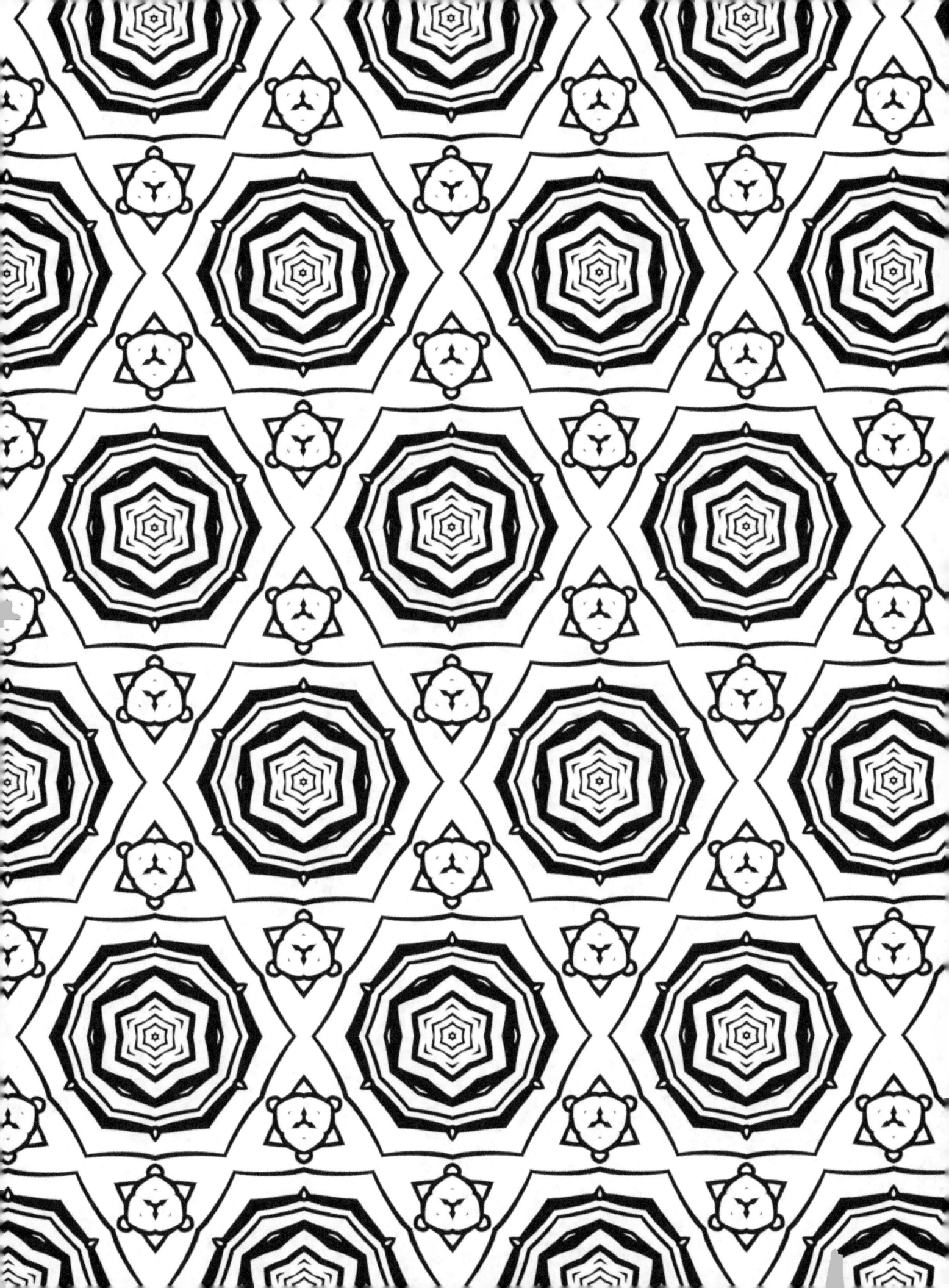

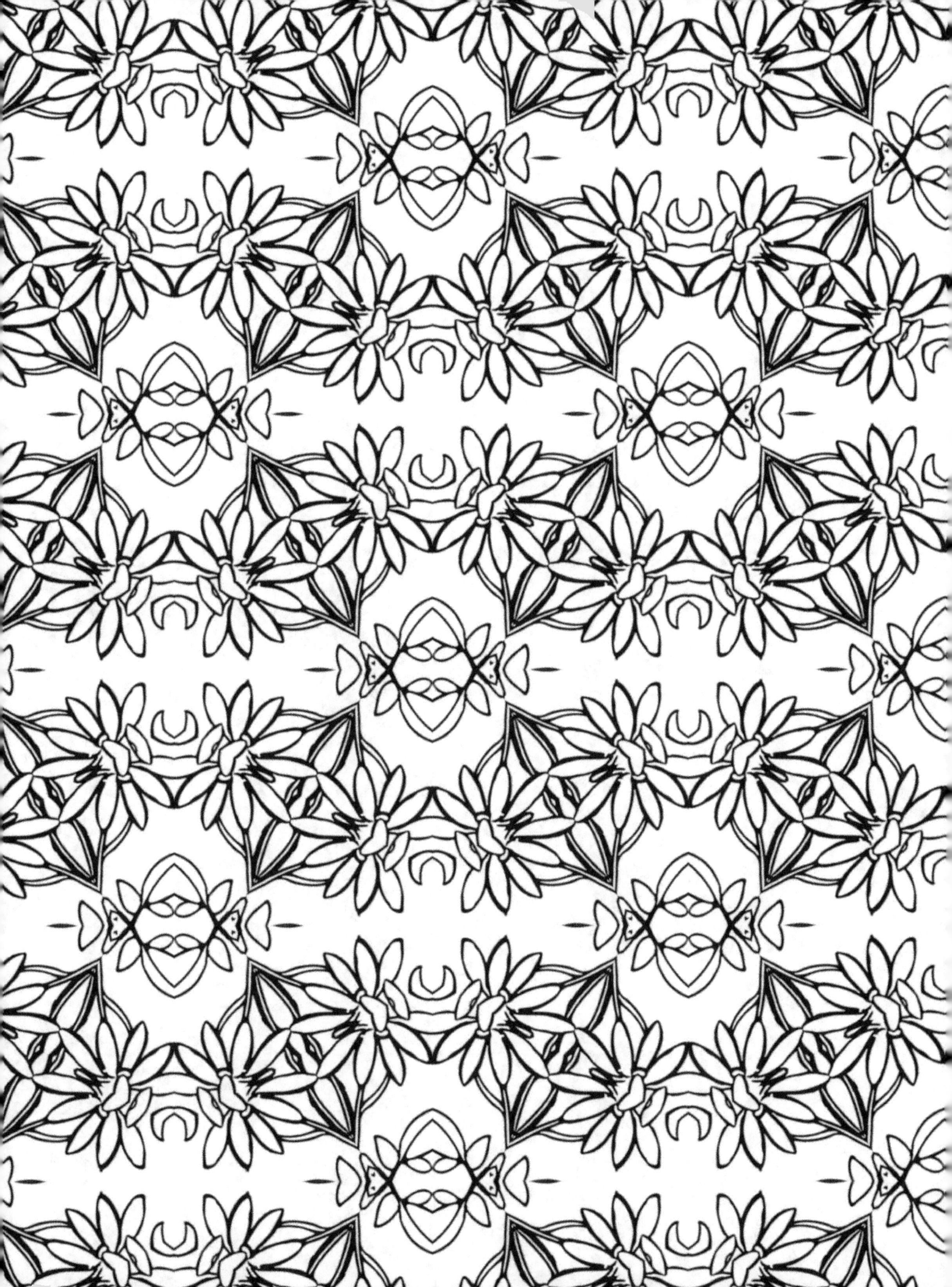

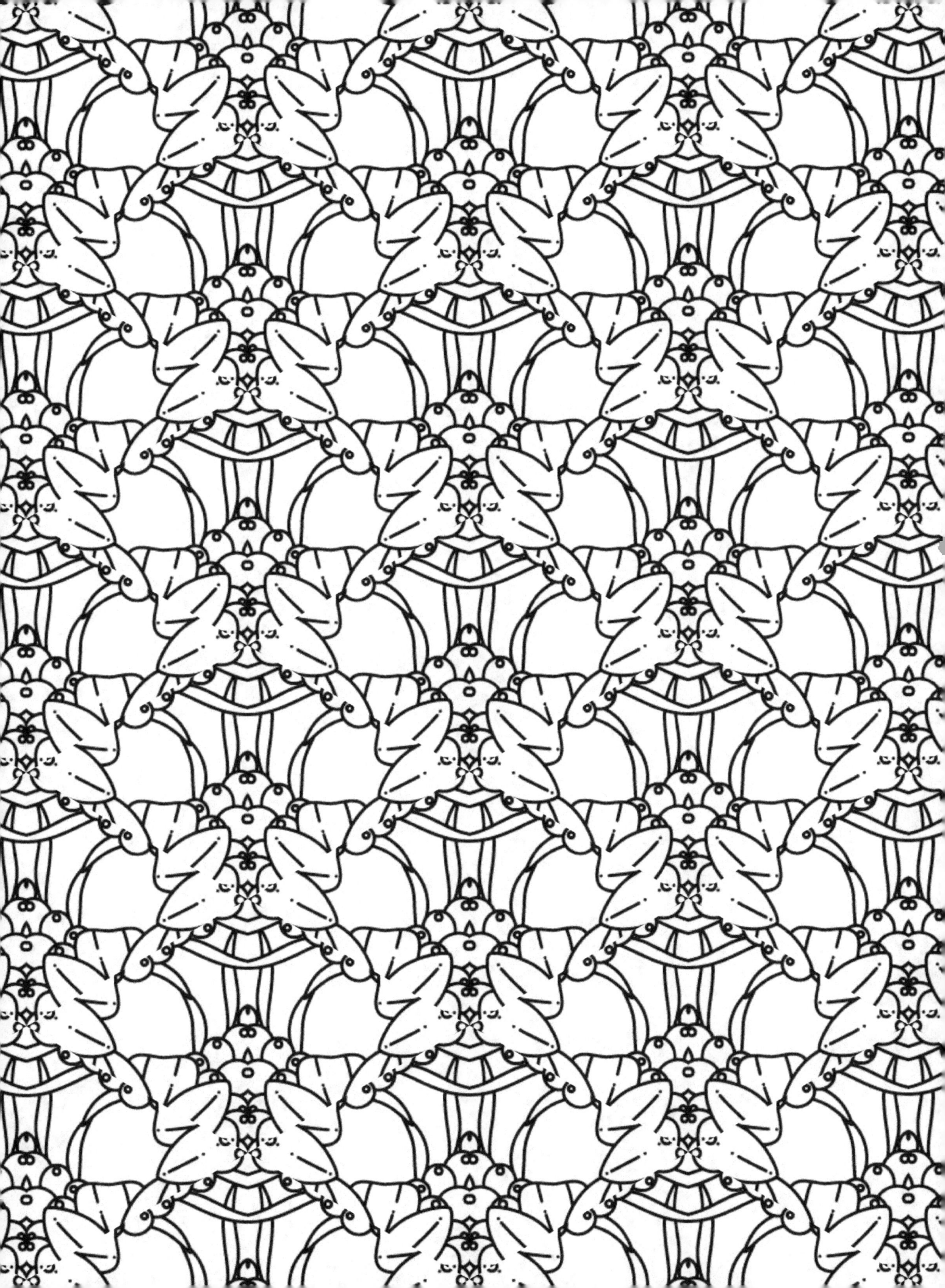

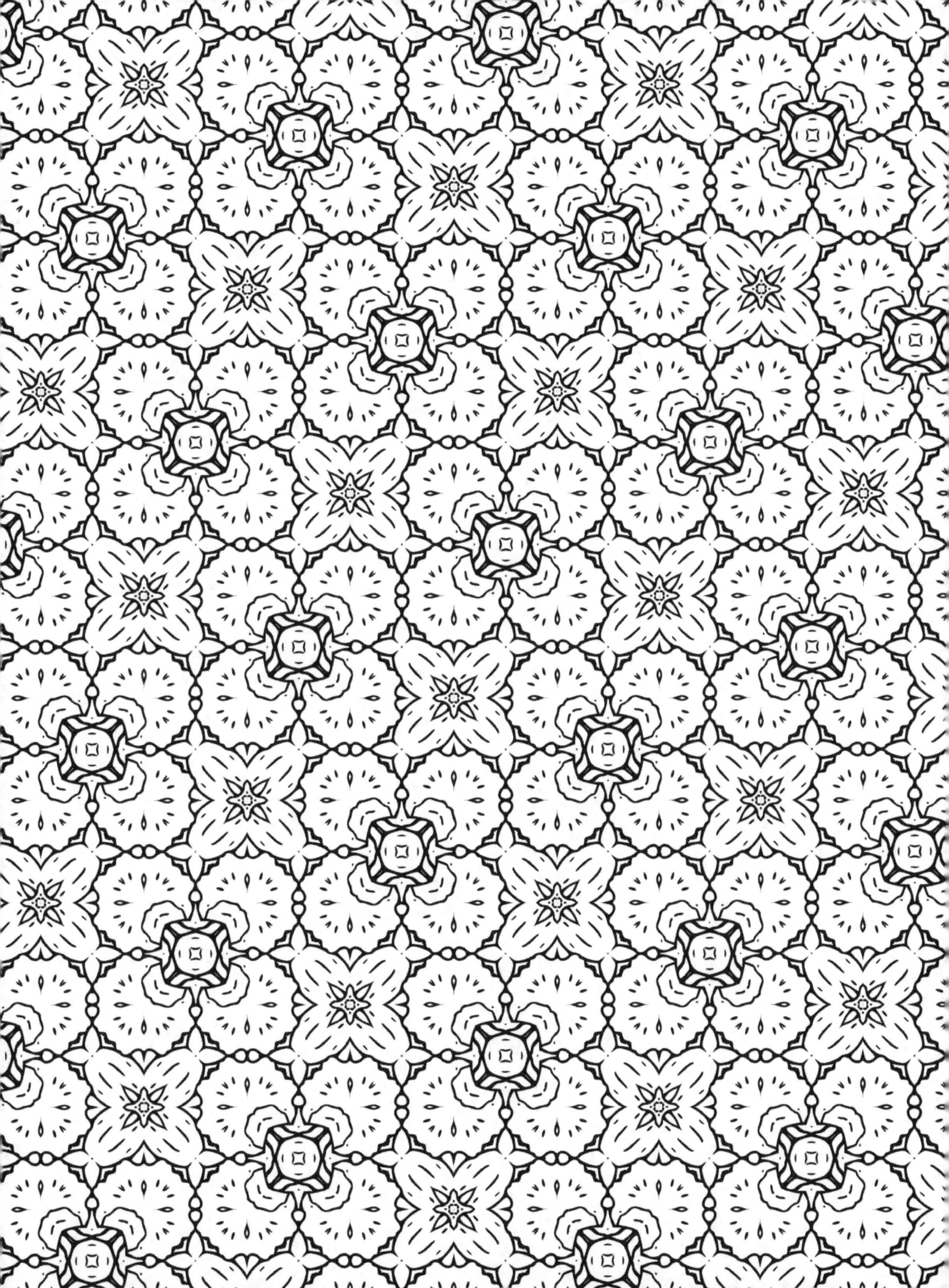

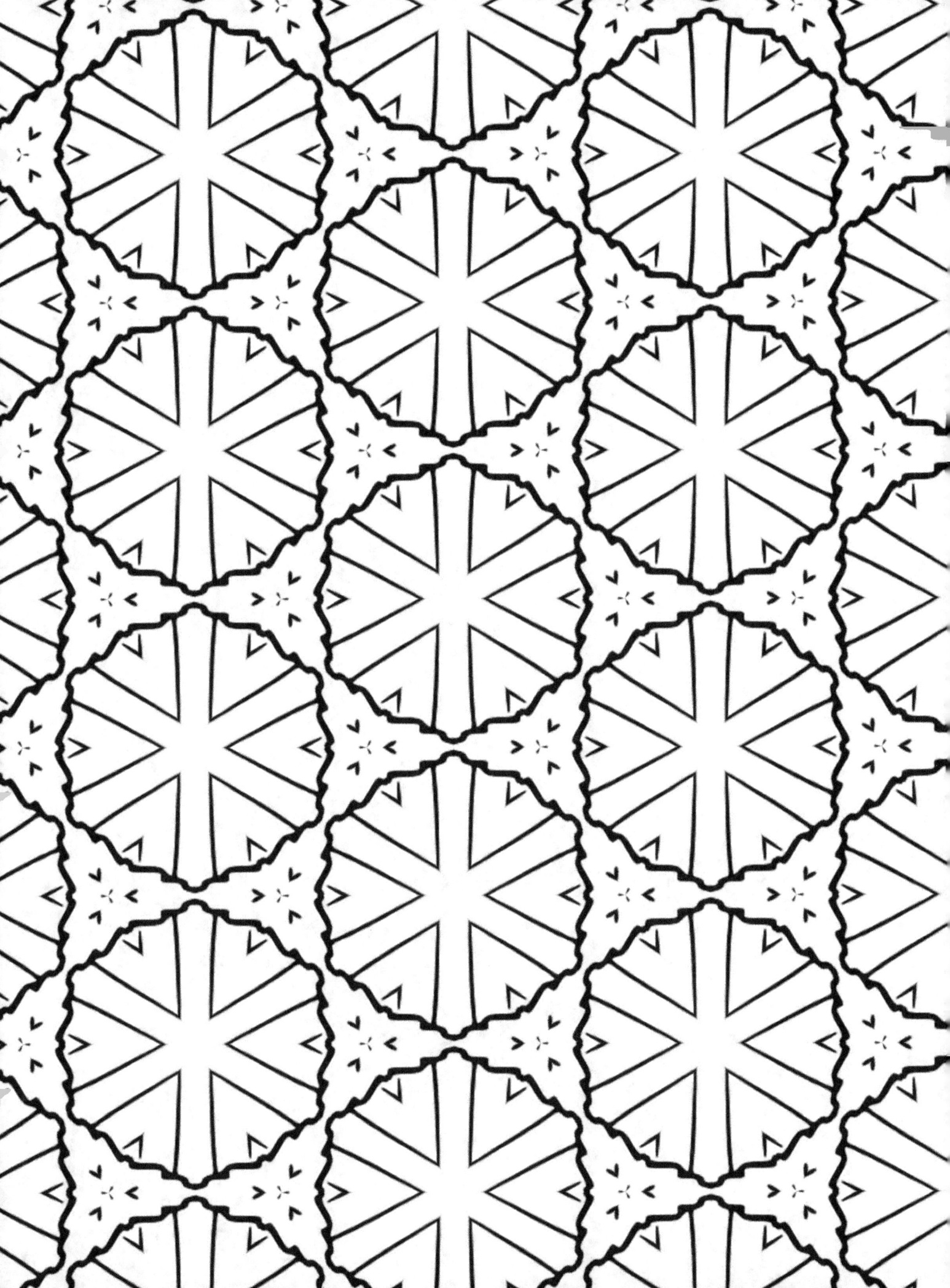

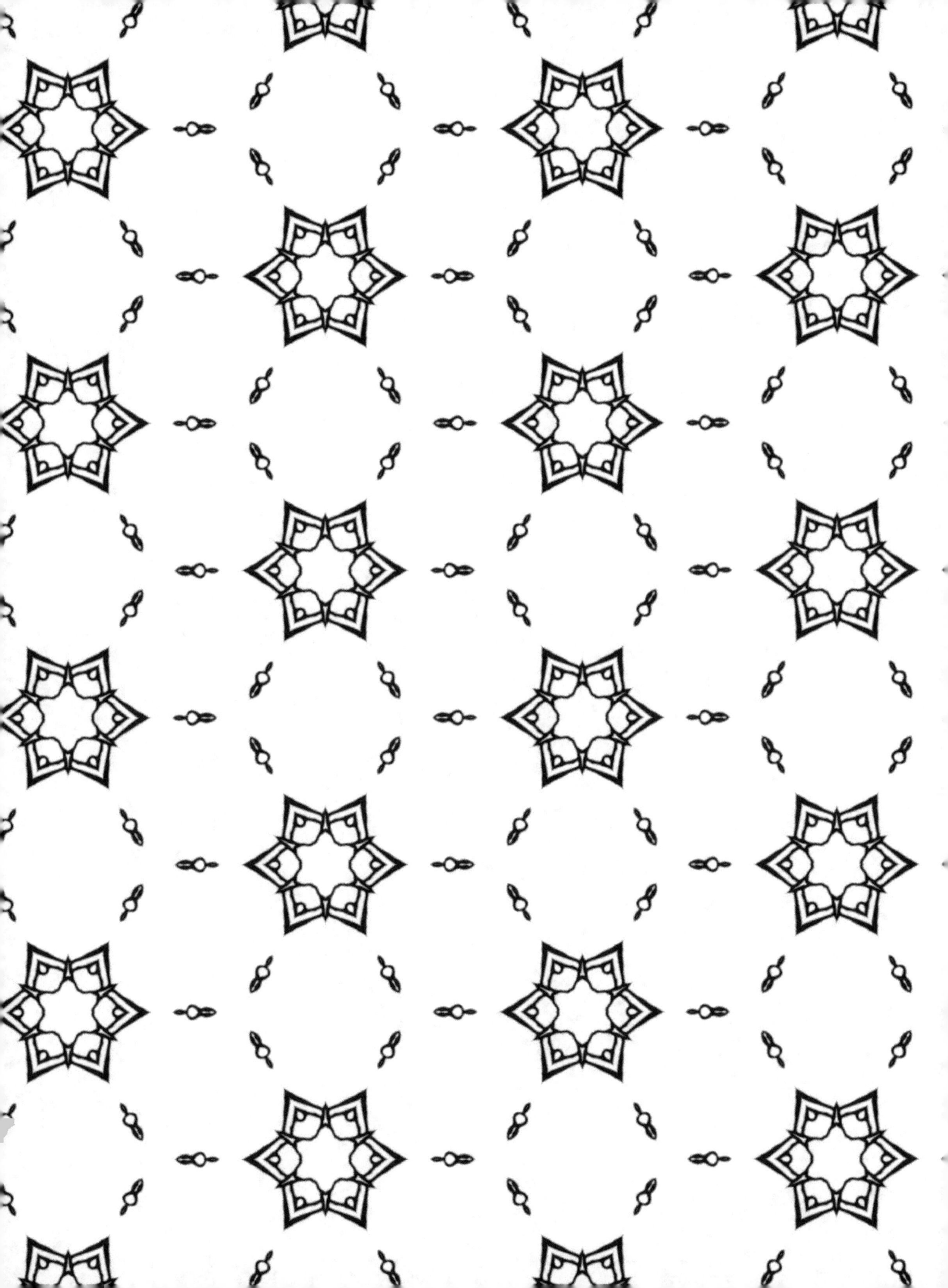

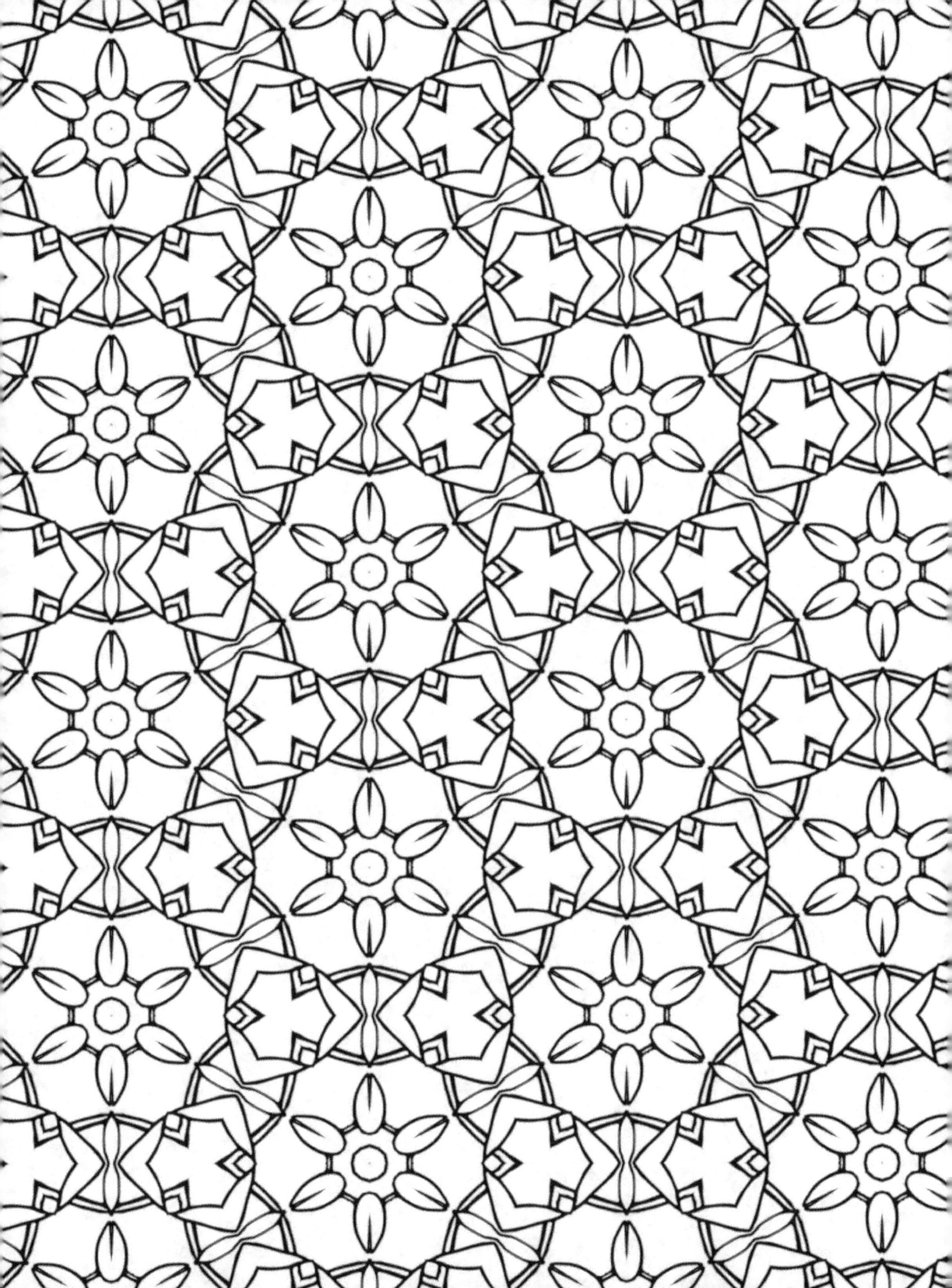

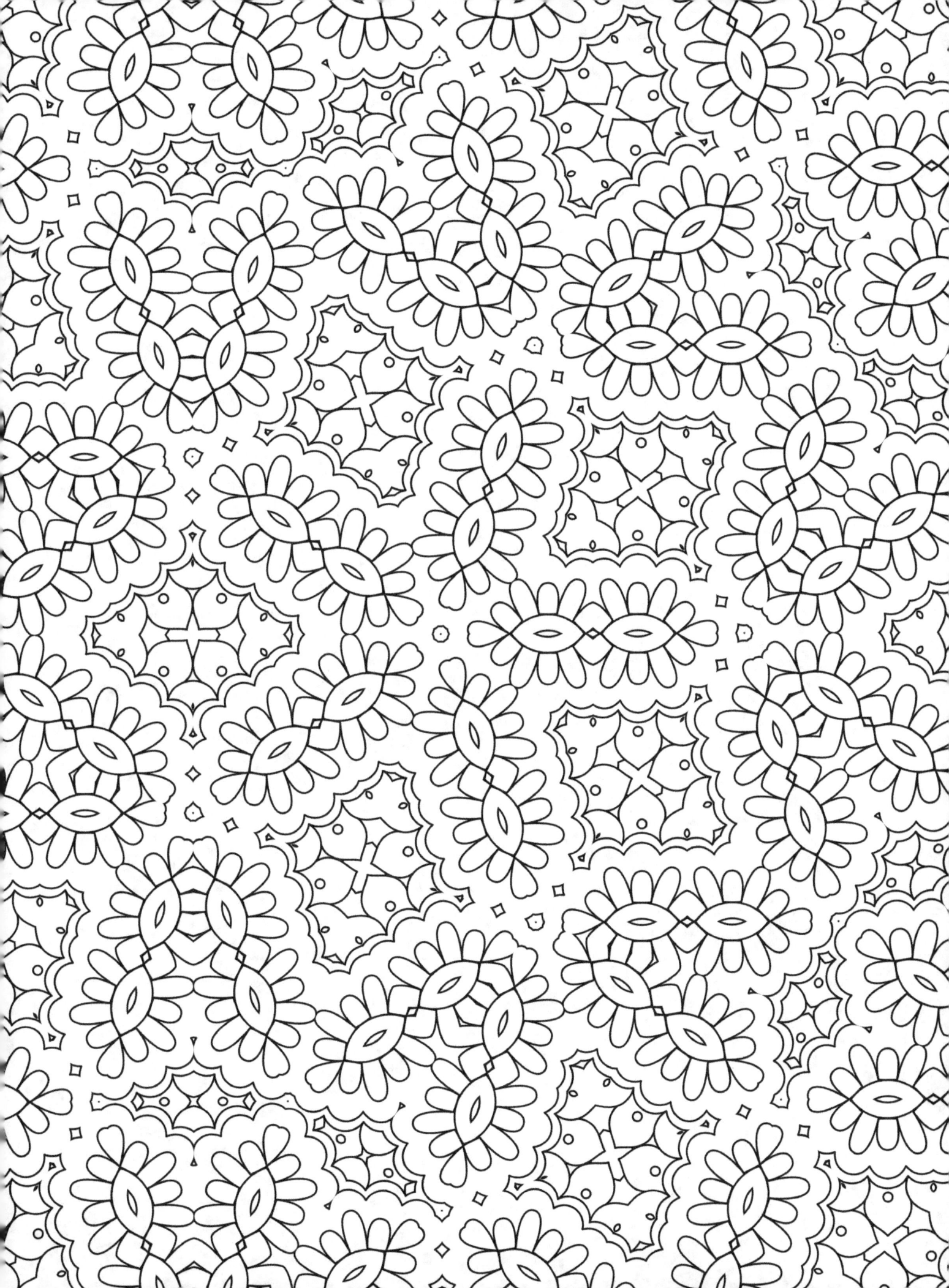

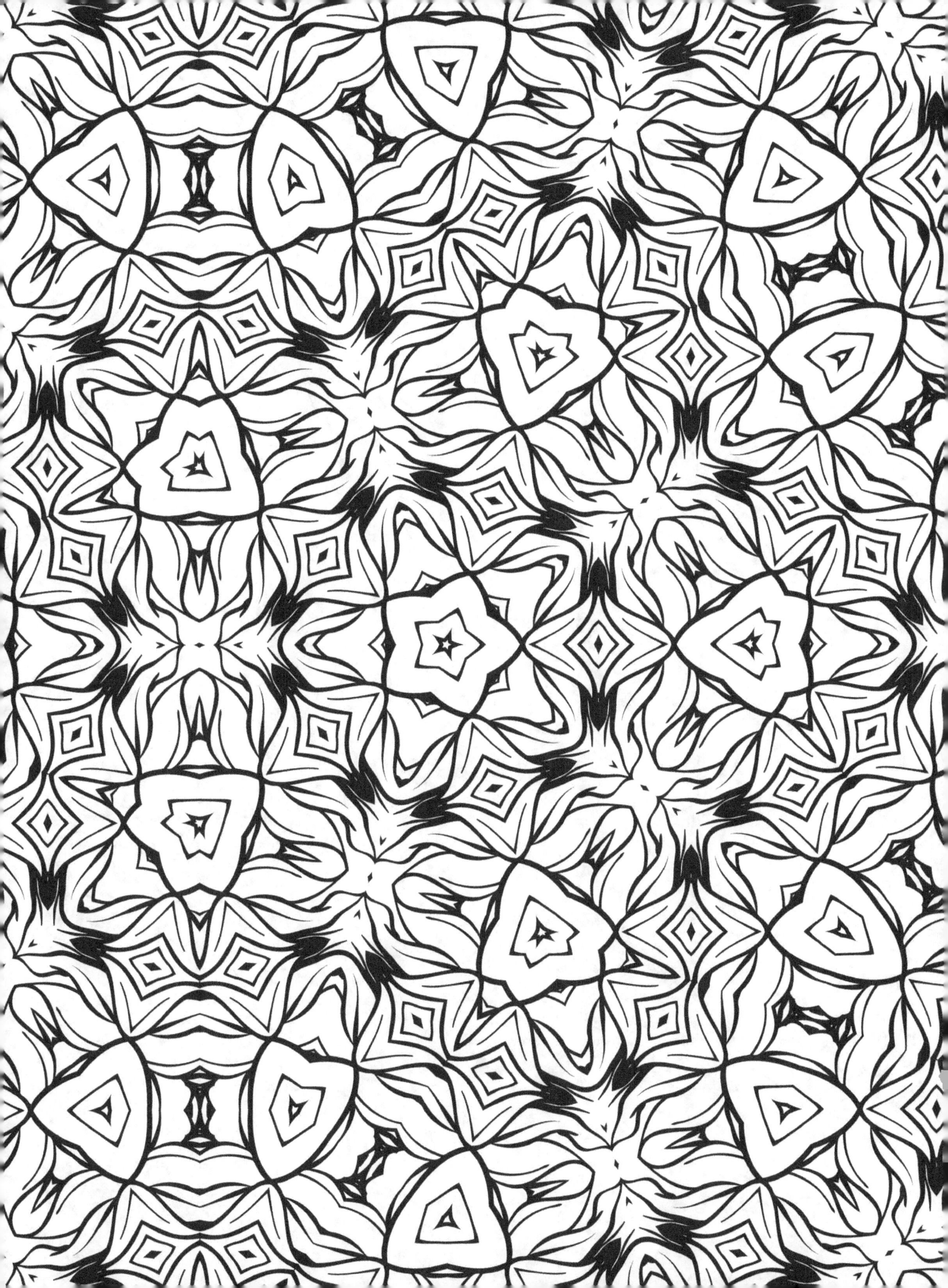

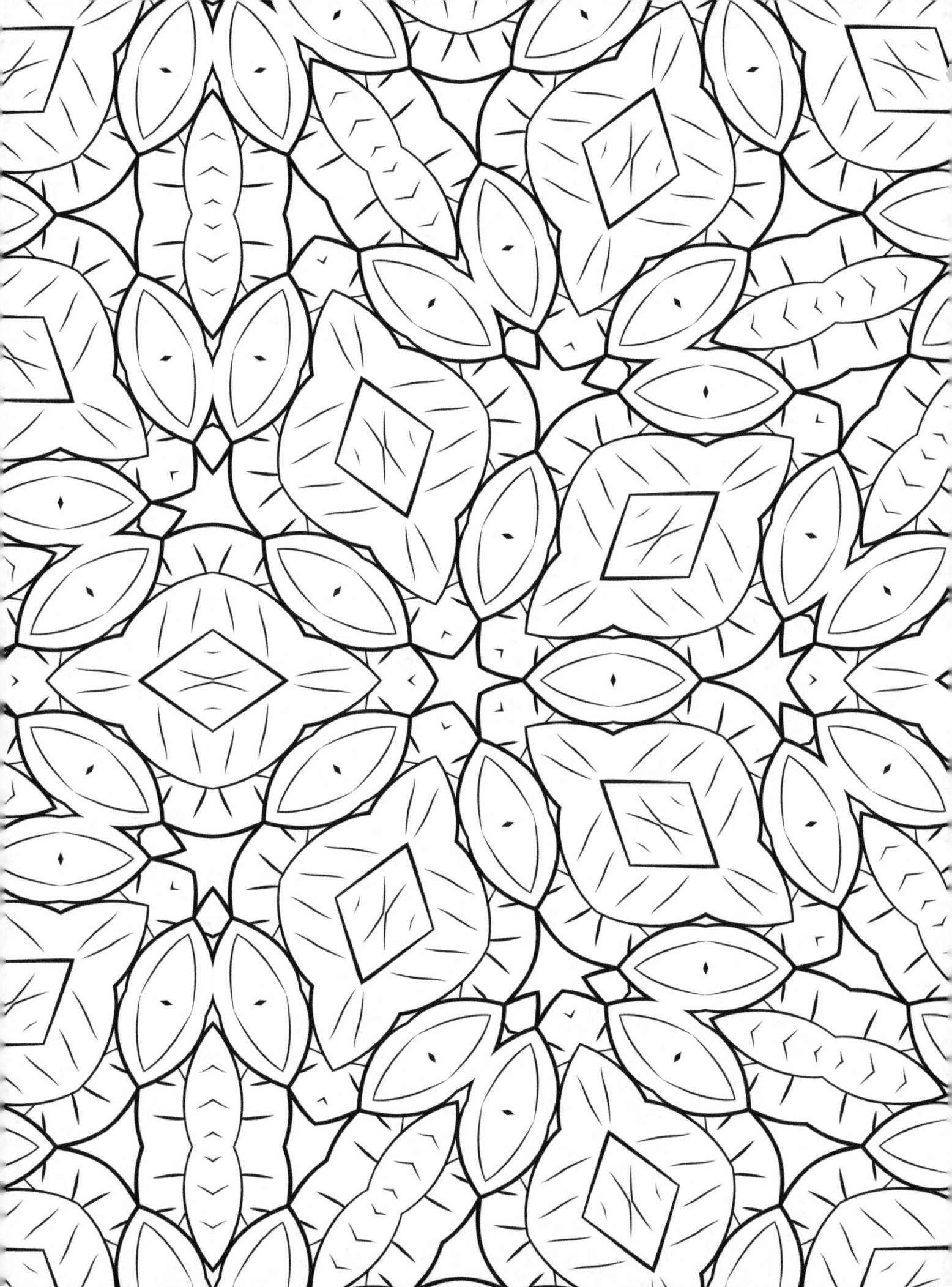

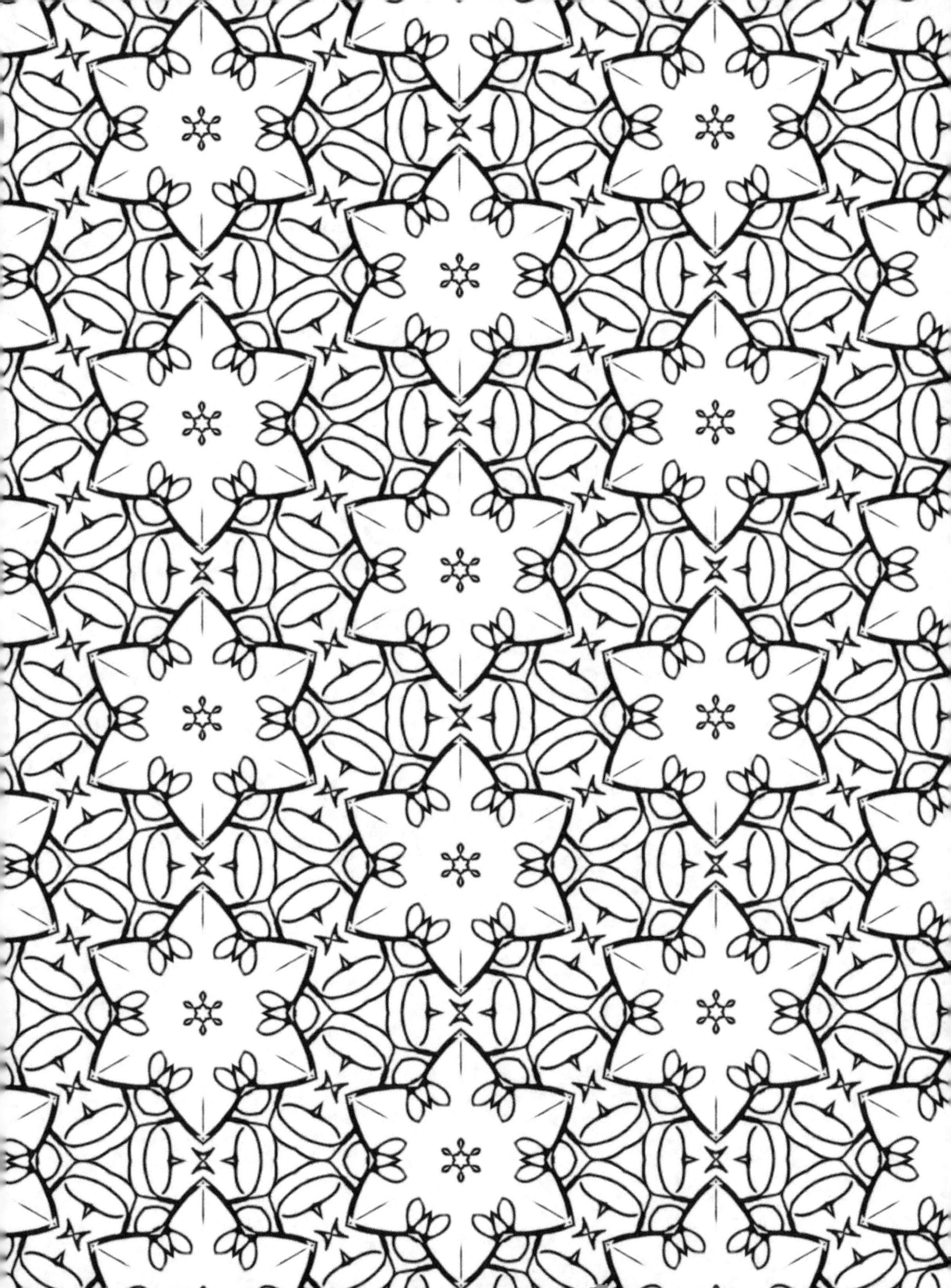

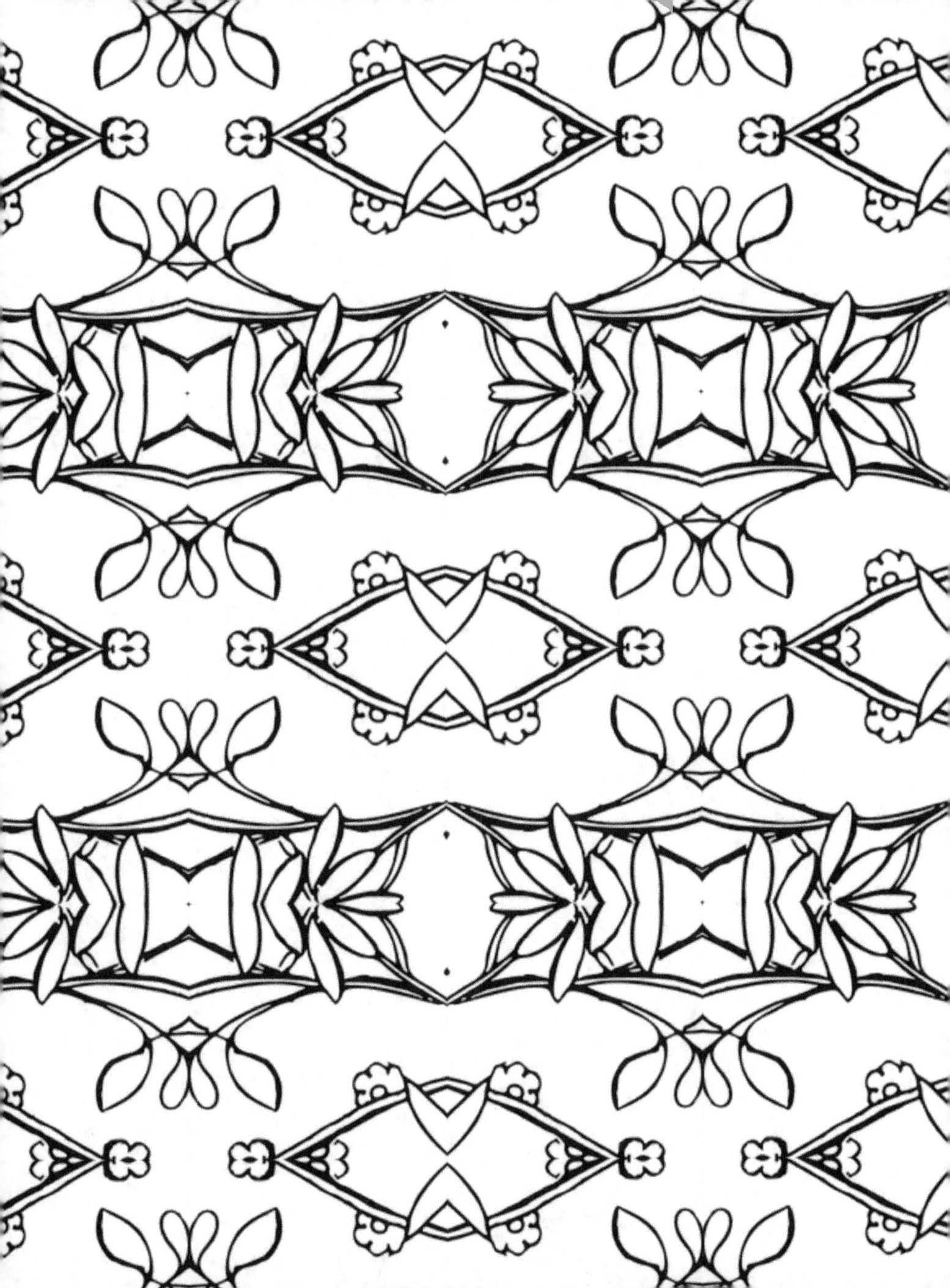

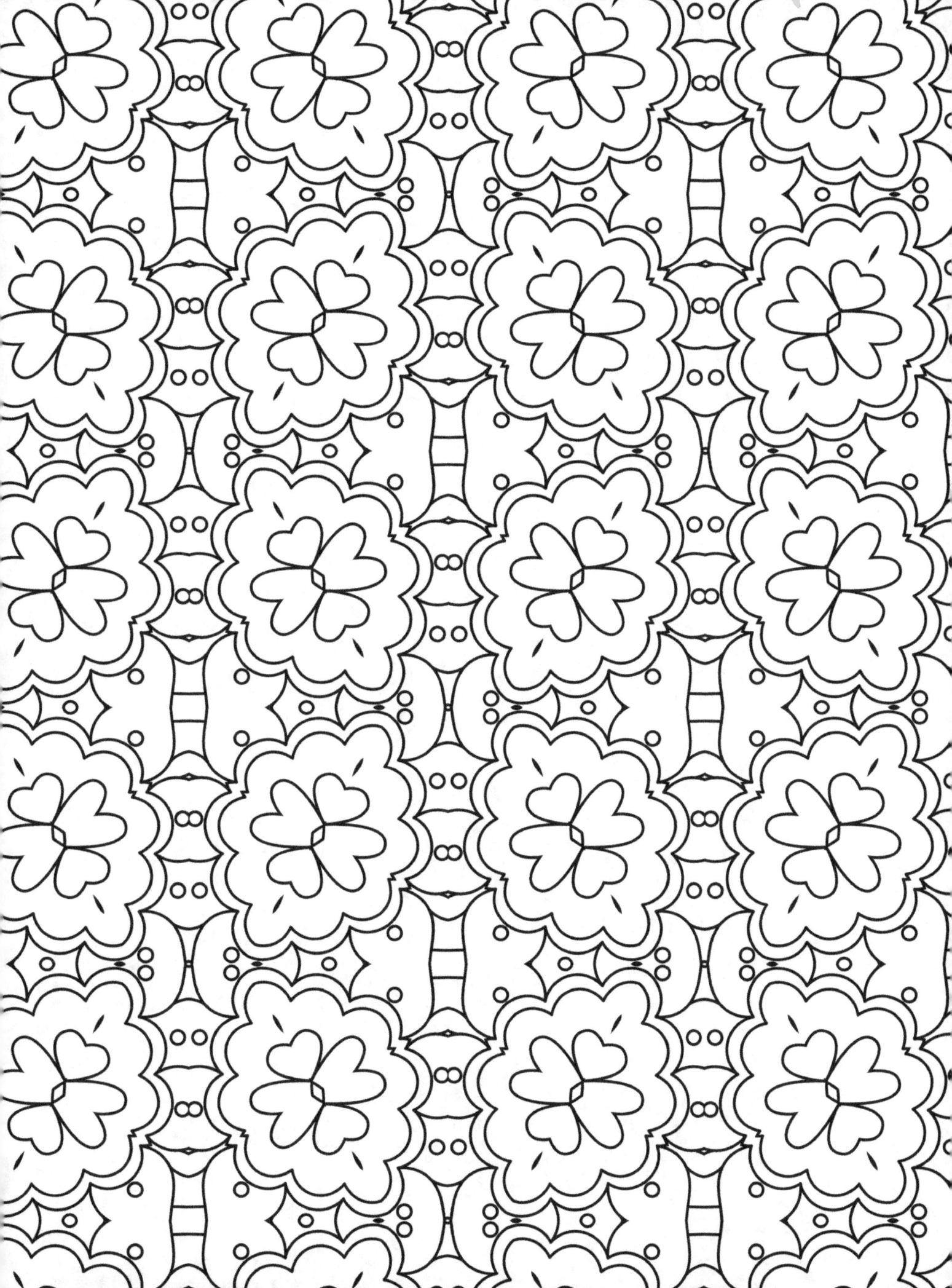

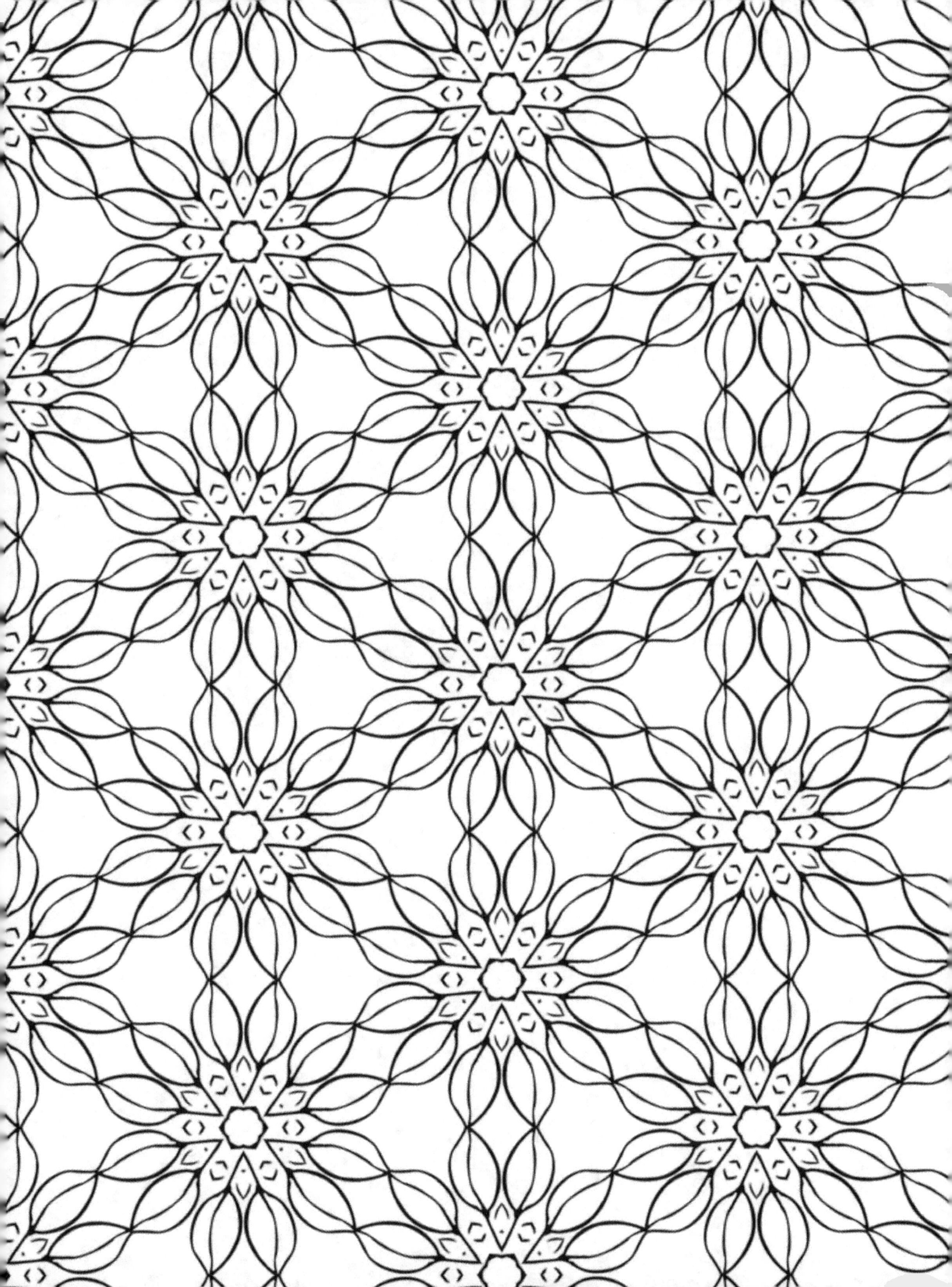

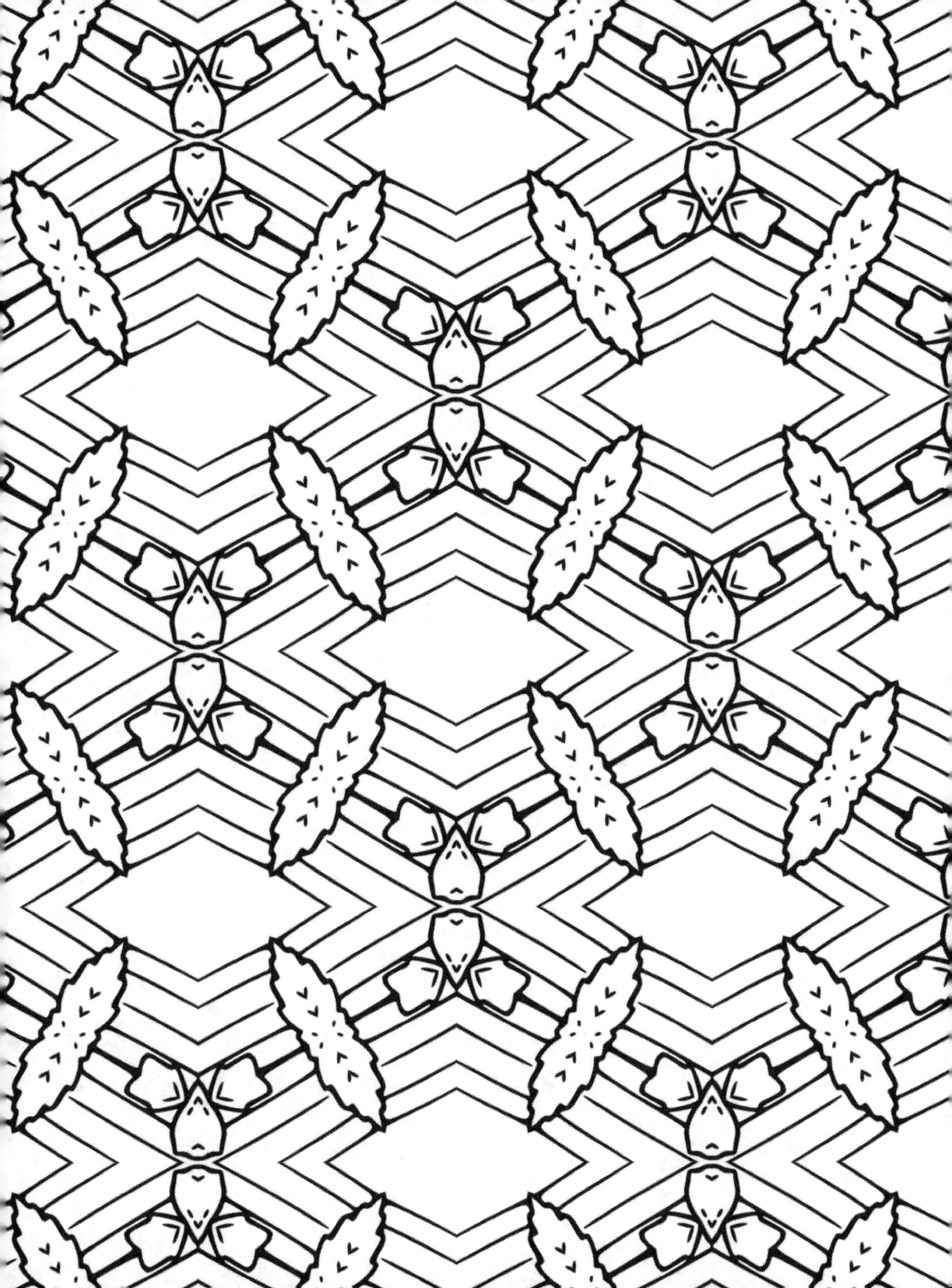

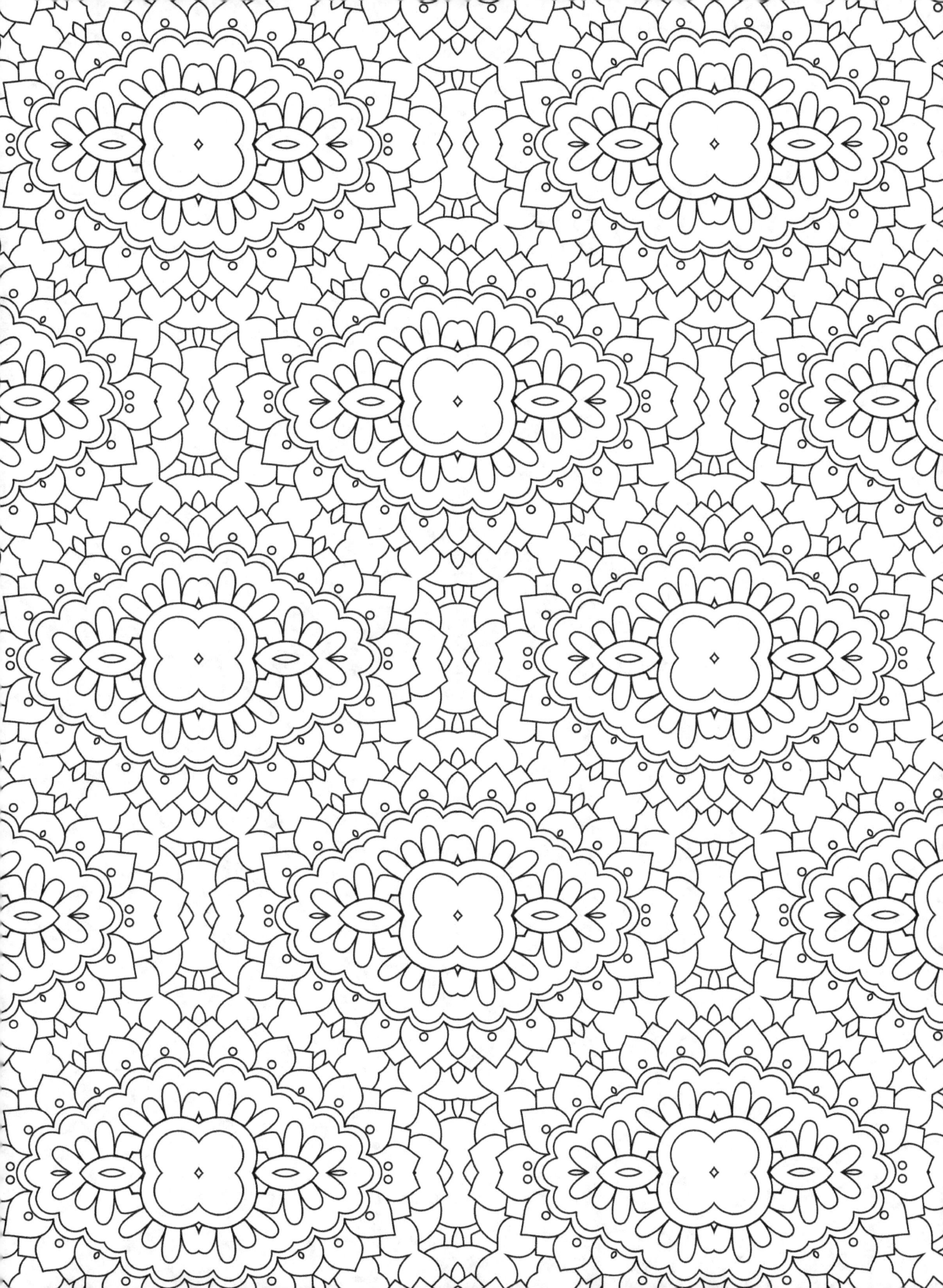

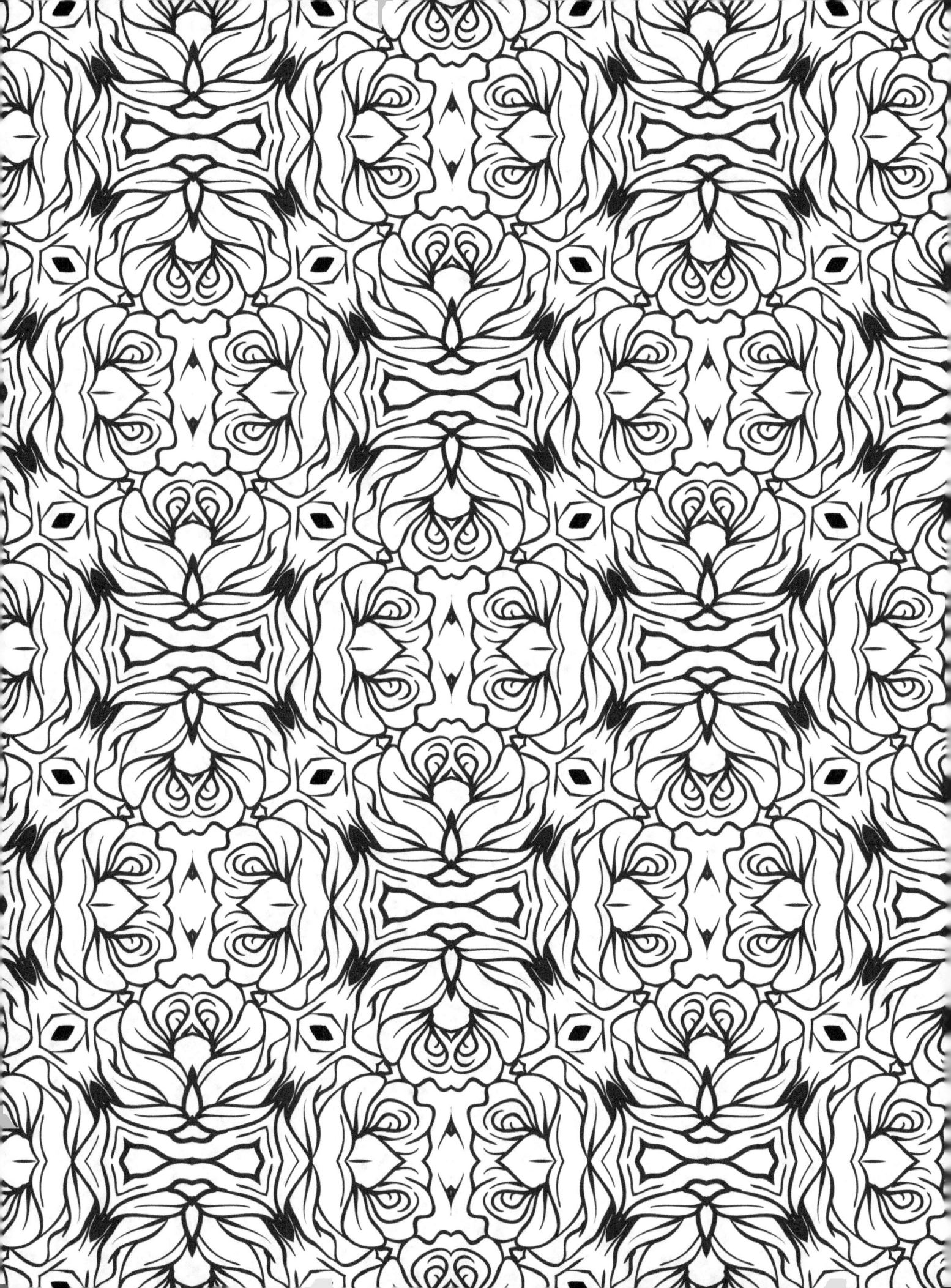

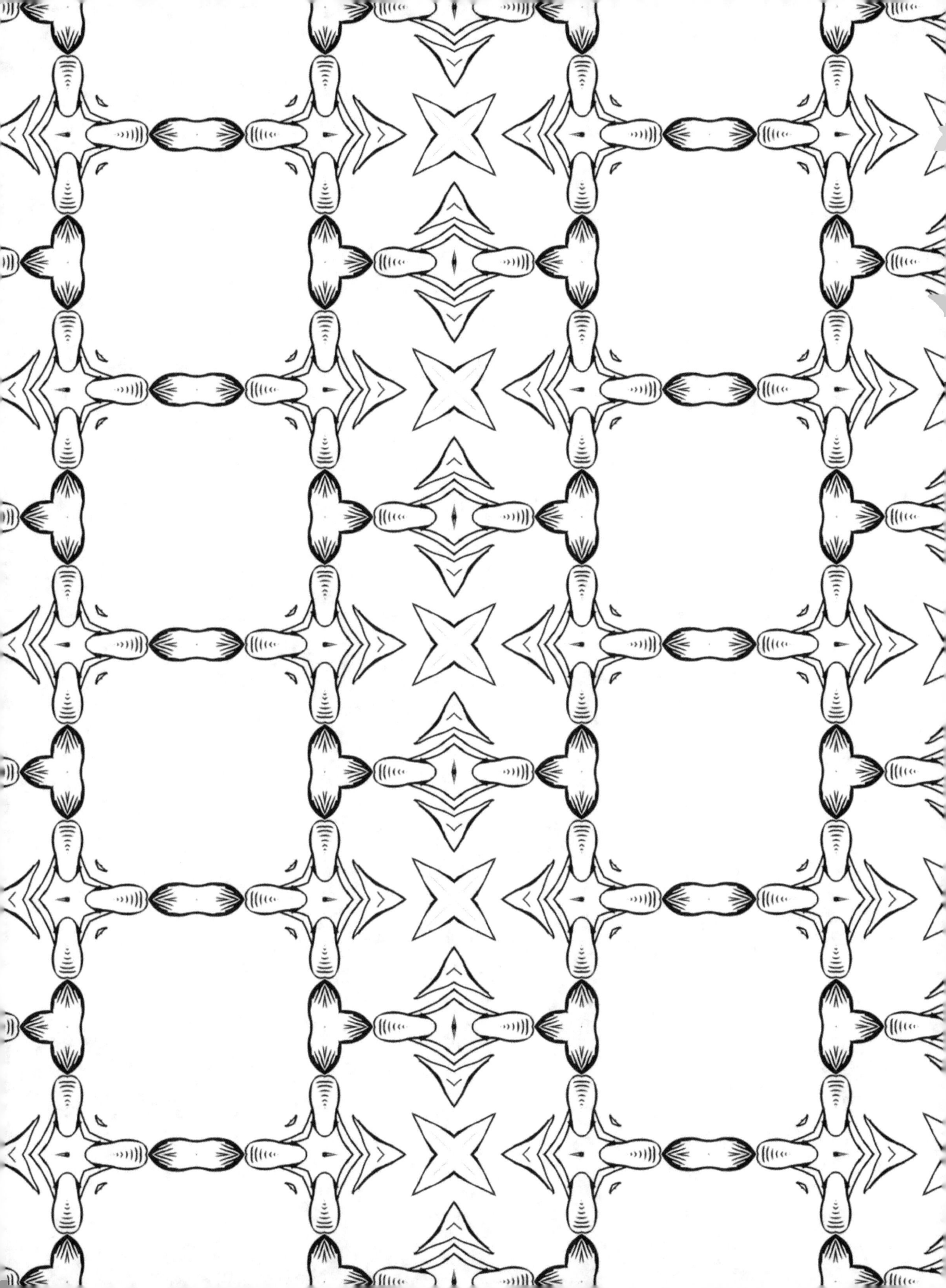

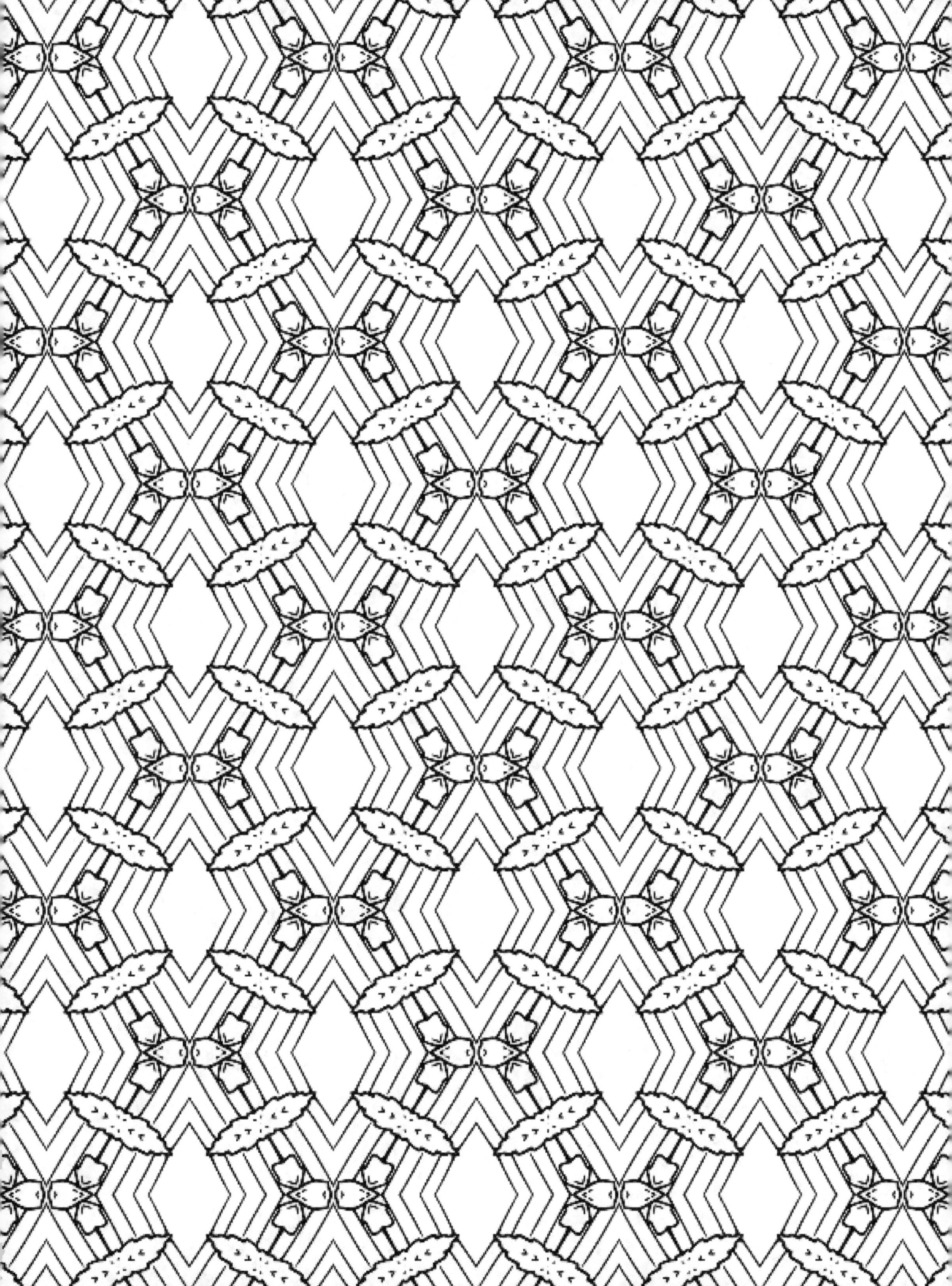

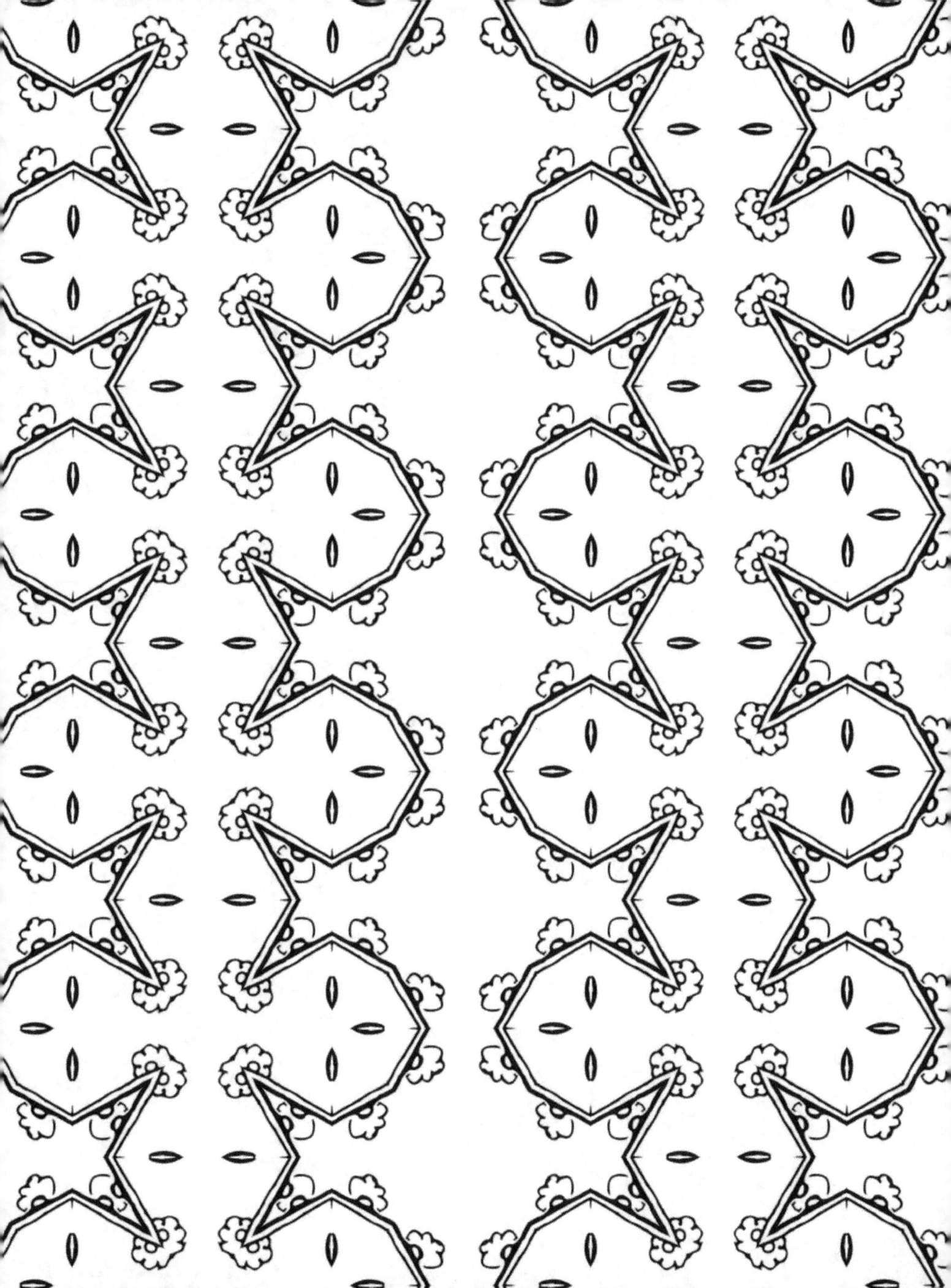

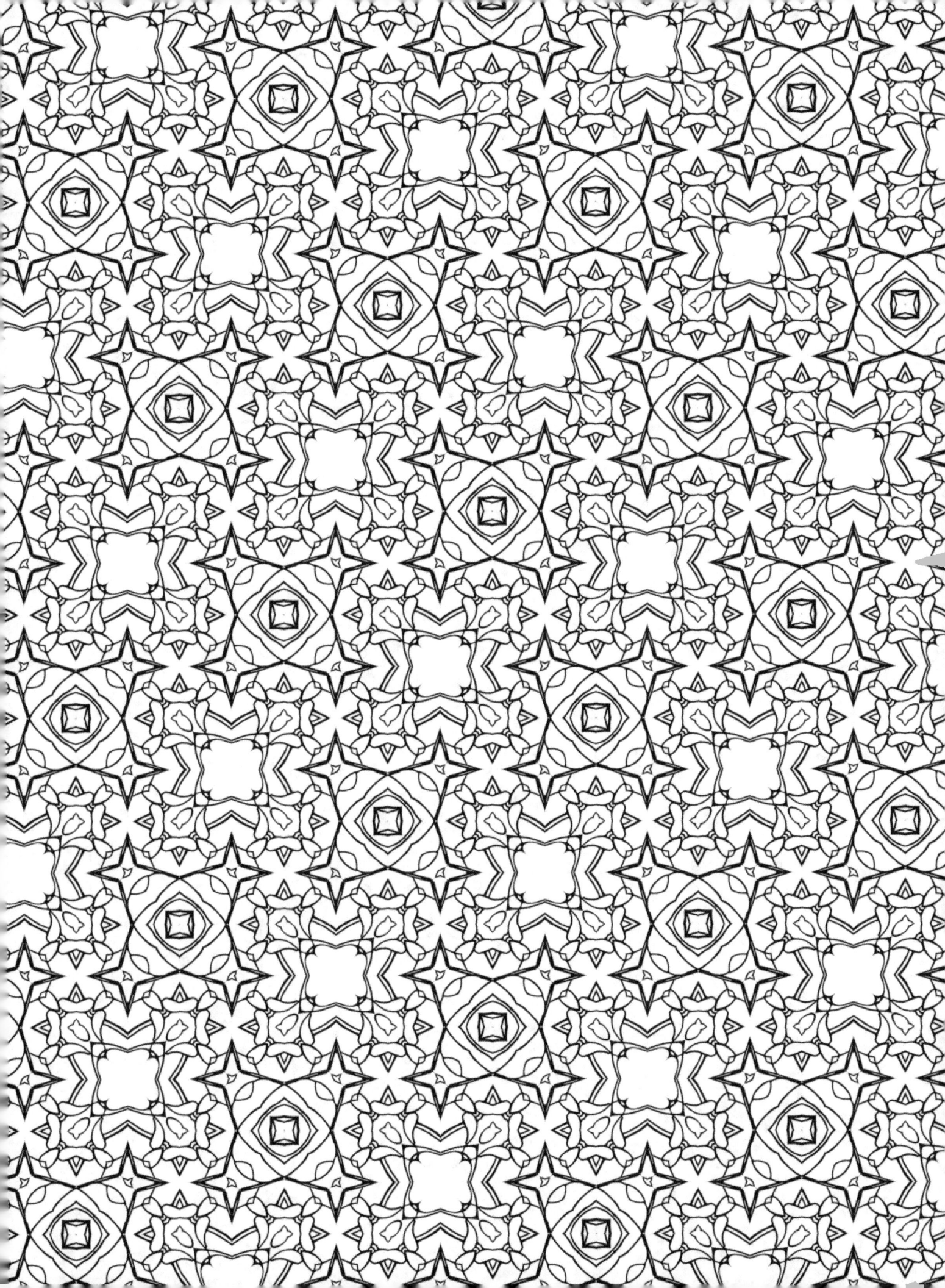

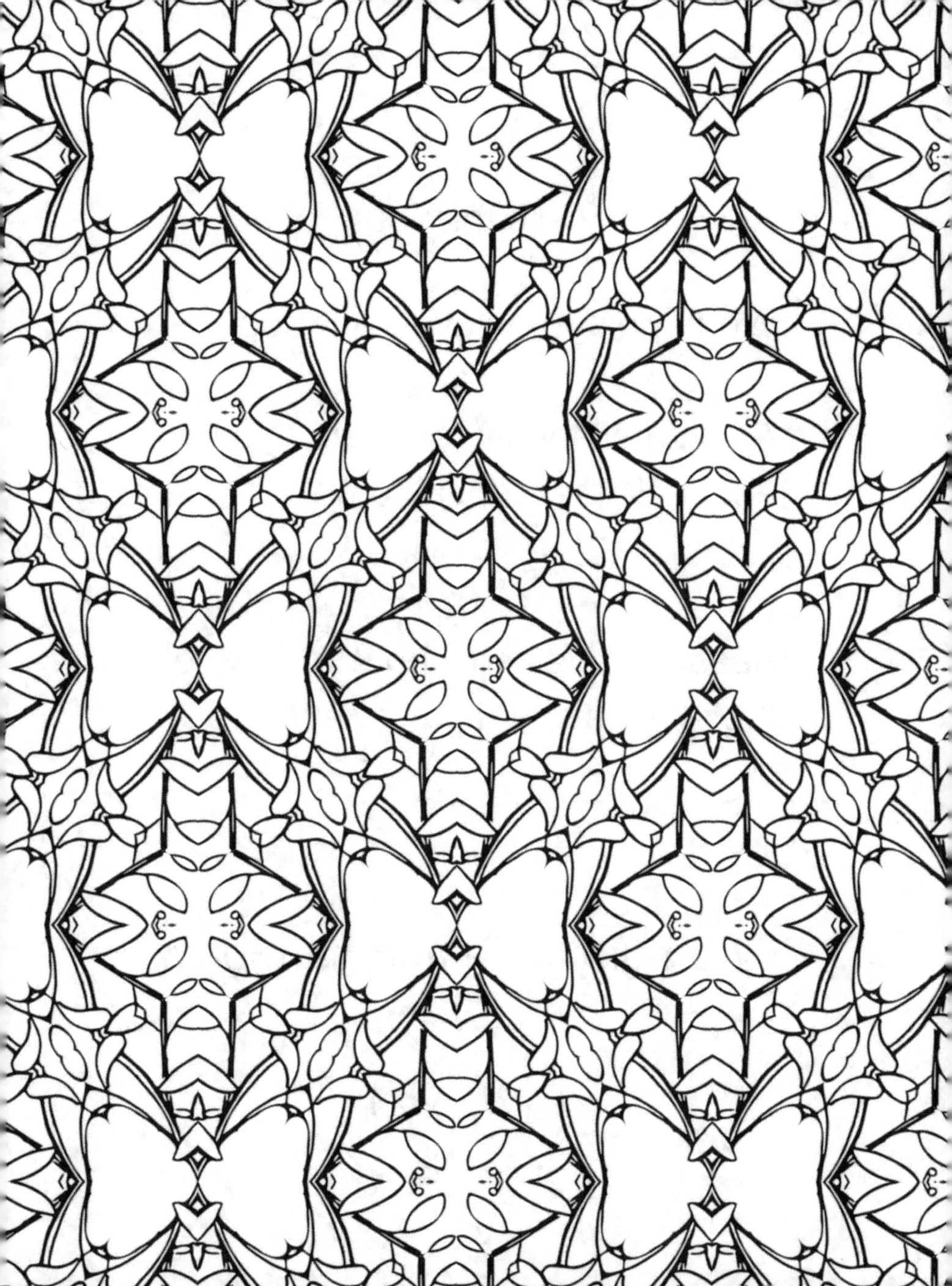

Thank you!

We hope you enjoyed our book.

As a small family company, your feedback is essential to us.

Please, let us know how you like our book by leaving us a review.

With gratitude and harmony,

Dalu

www.ingramcontent.com/pod-product-compliance
Lightning Source LLC
Chambersburg PA
CBHW080936220526

45465CB00008BA/3070